souls like ourselves

Because they are so closely akin to us and share our
unknowingness, I loved all warm-blooded animals
who have souls like ourselves and with whom, so I
thought, we have an instinctive understanding.

Dr. Carl G. Jung

Souls Like Ourselves
Inspired Thoughts for Personal and Planetary Advancement

Edited by
Andrea Gillan Wiebers, M.S.W.
and David O. Wiebers, M.D.

Sojourn
press

Rochester, Minnesota

Library of Congress Card Number: 99-90255
ISBN Number: 0-9670979-0-8

For information, write:
Sojourn Press
P.O. Box 6456
Rochester, MN 55903-6456

Or call:
(507) 288-4370

Or e-mail:
SojournPrs@aol.com

Discounts for organizations are available.

Book design
Heaton Brandt Communications, Edina, MN

Watercolor paintings
Andrea Gillan Wiebers

Printed in the United States on acid-free, recycled paper with soy ink.

1st edition

10 9 8 7 6 5 4 3 2 1

Contents

PREFACE

Preface

When a human is born, his or her first and foremost concern is with personal comfort and safety. Usually, with appropriate attention and coaching, this concern and priority gradually extends to include one's parents followed by one's immediate family. From there, as a child grows and learns to grant to others the same feelings and awareness achieved for his or her own self, the circle of compassion widens.

Although this learning process is greatly facilitated by internal predisposition, it is not automatic. The extent to which humans are externally encouraged to see beyond themselves and are taught to recognize the independent value of other beings is, in part, a matter of parental and societal influence. This influence can be directed at breaking down barriers of difference, teaching people that behind the externalities of nationality, race, gender, economic and social class, religion and ethnicity, there exists in the other a consciousness and a set of yearnings that demand uncompromising respect. The next logical step in the pathway is to extend one's compassion and caring to species other than humans. Our society is in the process of awakening to the significance of this step so that it might evolve to the next level.

Throughout recorded history, there have been luminaries who have been far ahead of the rest of humanity with a deep understanding of the significance of compassion for all life. The written and spoken words of these enlightened individuals can be both fascinating and inspiring, and can help light the way for all of us.

In this book, we have sought to bring together a collection of quotations from a host of such individuals, who, by their words and deeds, reflect a deeper understanding of the value of all life. These individuals have come from numerous walks of life and their wisdom was, in many cases, not fully comprehended or appreciated during their lifetimes. It is our sincere hope that the readers of this book will also be inspired by these passages and that any one of them may serve as a starting point for those who are searching for meaning and for ways to make themselves and the world better.

Note

The quotations in this volume were compiled from a wide variety of sources. Thus, varying amounts of information were available regarding each quotation and author. Every effort has been made to reproduce this information accurately. Undoubtedly, there are many quotable individuals whose words have not yet come to our attention. We welcome any suggestions or additions from readers for future editions, sent to Sojourn Press.

Introduction

One of the most compelling aspects of extending one's compassion to species other than humans involves the sheer magnitude of suffering among animals that takes place on a day-to-day basis, much of it occurring at the hands of humans. When one looks at the sum total of sentient beings on this earth who have experienced unnecessary death and suffering, the vast majority involves animals.

Why does the death and suffering of beings other than humans matter so much to a physician and a social worker?

In the health and human services arenas, one is continuously mindful of the value and sacredness of human life and of the virtue in promoting and enhancing it. This applies not only to the most intelligent and articulate human beings, but also to the least fortunate among us, including those with severe acquired illnesses and developmental defects, some of which may be so profound as to preclude meaningful communication with others.

Each individual has a unique value, not by virtue of his or her level of intelligence or ability to communicate in a certain way, but by virtue of the energy inhabiting that body that instills recognizable "life" into its protoplasm. This energy, which activates the human brain, allows the physical structures of the brain to achieve consciousness, make decisions, think thoughts, and feel pain and pleasure. Without such energy, the human body (including the brain) is merely a carcass devoid of these capabilities.

Although scientists are attempting to develop the technology to measure this energy directly, there is currently no consistent way to do so. We can, however, measure many of its consequences. For example, from an electrophysiological standpoint, cerebral electrical activity can be measured via the electroencephalogram (EEG).

The similarity between this energy in the human and that in other animals is, upon reflection, self-evident, particularly for those who have closely associated with animals and observed their personalities carefully over many years. Even without such careful observation, logic would dictate that the life-conferring energy allowing consciousness, thoughts, decisions, pain perception, etc., must reside in other living animals in order to activate their central nervous systems as it resides in living humans.

If more evidence is needed, the EEGs of animals are analogous to those of humans; in fact, the EEGs of gorillas and other primates are nearly indistinguishable from those of humans. This is not surprising given that the brain structure and other central and peripheral nervous system structures and circuitry, down to the cellular level, are analogous in humans and other animals, particularly primates, where again they may be almost indistinguishable. These structures include centers for motor function; associated motor movements; sensory systems for pain and touch perception, vision, hearing, taste, and smell; and, in many cases, centers that mediate mood and personality.

There has been a general tendency among humans, and a specific inclination among scientists and theologians, to draw a very sharp line between humans and other animals while disregarding significant analogies and areas of overlap. As a result, ethical standards have been developed with little or no consideration for sentient beings other than humans, based on certain features possessed by humans but not other animals.

Scientists have usually focused upon the superiority of human intelligence or language function. Yet gorillas and other primates have scored higher on intelligence tests designed by and for humans than have some humans. Almost all animals have some form of easily recognizable communication, and it is now clear that at least some primates can be taught sign language and other forms of language, though none yet can master our exact vocabulary. These animals possess more language function than a child who is less than three months old and considerably more function that a human born without cerebral hemispheres who cannot meaningfully interact with the environment or other beings. Although the latter may survive with a life-force energy activating his or her central nervous system, limitations of the brain restrict the capacity of this energy to express itself.

Theologians have historically drawn the line between humans and other animals with the underlying premise that animals cannot possess souls or spirits. Yet it is precisely this life-force energy in humans, constituting the soul or spirit, that must also inhabit and activate the central nervous systems of other living animals. Virtually all of the world's major spiritual traditions and a growing collection of scientific data on near-death experiences and related phenomena suggest the capacity for this energy, soul, or spirit to transcend (exist separately from) the human body. The primary definition of soul in *Webster's New World Dictionary* is "an entity which is regarded as being the immortal or spiritual part of the person, and though having no physical or material reality, is credited with the functions of thinking and willing, and hence, determining all behavior." If, in the preceding sentence the word, "person" were changed to "individual," the resulting definition would fit clearly with what we know about other animals as well as humans.

Few would deny that the mentally retarded child, or even the child born without cerebral hemispheres, has a soul or spirit, yet there has been a reluctance on the part of many to accept that this possibility exists in animals. We humans should be open to the further possibility that the differences we observe between humans and animals may not relate as much to the energy/soul/spirit that inhabits the bodies and brains of humans and other animals as they do to the bodies and brains themselves, which specifically define and limit the expression of this energy. A parallel phenomenon can be observed in humans with various impairments. It hardly seems possible that the energy or soul residing within a human who has a stroke or contracts Alzheimer's disease is somehow eternally destroyed or damaged. On the contrary, that part of all of us that is immortal or capable of transcending the body should not be damaged by illness or any other structural change to the human body, but rather its expression temporarily limited.

Clearly, there are distinct and major differences between humans and other animals. However, we should not be too quick to judge the significance of these differences since there is a considerable amount of evidence to suggest that, even by human definitions, the most important and enduring elements in humans and animals may be those elements that differ the least.

Other physicians and scientists have made similar observations about the minds of humans and other animals. The eminent British neurologist Lord Walter Russell Brain (1895-1966) observed, "I personally can see no reason for conceding mind to my fellow man and denying it to animals...I at least cannot doubt that the interests and activities of animals are correlated with awareness and feeling in the same way as my own." Nearly a century earlier, in his book *The Descent of Man*, Charles Darwin (1809-1882) observed, "There is no fundamental difference between man and the higher mammals in their mental faculties. The difference in mind between man and higher animals, great as it is, is certainly one of degree and not of kind."

As we reflect upon these observations, we cannot help but feel a sense of great obligation, not only to other human life but to non-human life as well. Humankind's superior intelligence and capacity for making moral judgments do not confer upon us the right to exploit other species (or for that matter other humans with lesser intellectual capacity) but rather a responsibility to show compassion for them and assist them.

One cannot help but wonder how we humans would react if an intellectually superior race of beings with advanced telepathic communication capabilities we could not comprehend were to land on Earth. Would they be morally justified on the basis of these additional capabilities to utilize humans in the ways we currently utilize other animals for the benefit of their "superior" race?

Dr. Albert Einstein (1879-1955) commented, "A human being...experiences himself, his thoughts, and feelings, as something separate from the rest, a kind of optical delusion of his consciousness....Our task must be to free ourselves from the prison by widening our circle of compassion to embrace all living creatures and the whole of nature and its beauty. Nobody is able to achieve this completely, but the striving for such achievement is in itself part of the liberation and a foundation for inner security."

While there is much that can yet be done to decrease human suffering, most humans have become aware of the virtue of not killing or torturing other humans and have learned to think of other humans as ends rather than means.

It has become generally accepted in our society that killing or otherwise causing suffering in other humans is unethical except in cases of self-defense in unavoidable situations. This applies regardless of the ends or economic impact, regardless of another human's ability to communicate in a certain way, and regardless of the amount of power that individual possesses.

With regard to animals, however, the above activities are condoned by much of society in a variety of venues unless they are applied to specific animals such as our own companion animals. The difference between one's companion animal and another animal that is raised for food or trapped in the wild parallels the difference between our human family members and humans from other families, cultures, or locations. Although most humans in our society recognize the virtue in not killing or otherwise causing suffering in companion animals, there continues to be a failure on the part of humankind as a whole to recognize the deeper identity of other animals, and, as a result, the same priorities have not been established for them. Consequently, to many, the mistreatment of these other sentient beings on such an enormous scale represents the widest gap in what would be an ideal world of harmony among earth's creatures and the world that currently exists.

A further aspect of extending the circle of one's compassion to other species, with great implications for contemporary society, is the direct, yet often unrecognized correlation between human-human and human-animal relationships. Mahatma Gandhi called attention to this when he said, "The greatness of a nation and its moral progress can be judged by the way its animals are treated." We would contend that an attitude reflecting compassion for all life is also the most crucial indicator of an individual's level of spiritual development. When humans show compassion toward others because the object of that compassion needs help rather than commands authority, it is the basis for peace on earth and peace within one's soul. If humankind can generally show compassion and a helping hand for other, less powerful species because it wants to, not because it has to, it will also be able to show these qualities more uniformly to all humans.

Throughout our tenure on this planet, humankind has searched for peace, most profoundly in the form of peace of mind. At the dawning of a new millennium humanity continues to search desperately for the keys to this elusive treasure, despite enormous technological advances and material wealth that miss the mark. Ultimately, the broader goal will be realized only after it becomes clear to enough of humanity that the journey to the inner peace it so desperately seeks must inevitably pass through the portal of "compassion for all life."

D.O.W.

souls like ourselves

1. COMPASSION, ETHICS AND NON-VIOLENCE

*S*ince we humans have the better brain, isn't it our responsibility to protect our fellow creatures from, oddly enough, ourselves?

Adamson, Joy (Author of *Born Free*), in *Woman's Almanac*, 1977

The pathway to Ahimsa [non-violence toward all living creatures] involves the most exciting journey a person can experience. It helps us tap our deepest sources of inspiration, truth and compassion. It helps us understand the essence of patience, of humor and of sharing the best we have to offer. The pathway helps us become integrated, aware and dynamic human beings who care about the world and want to make it a better place for all its citizens. Most of all, Ahimsa involves a unique process of creativity and enjoyment in living which will be reflected in everything we do.

Altman, Nathaniel, *Ahimsa*, 1980

The world stands at a parting of the ways and those who suffer know this with deeply anxious hearts. One way leads to destruction. It is the way of the tolerance of cruelty, if not the active engagement in it. It is the way of hunting for sport, the way of vivisection, the way of killing for self-adornment, the way of killing animals for food, the way of making slaves of animals without thought for their happiness and well-being. This is the way the world has been treading....The other way leads to salvation. It is the way of harmlessness, the way of the recognition of brotherhood with all creatures, the way of tenderness and compassion, the way of service and not of selfishness.

Arundale, George S., 1878-1945 (English theosophist), *The Night Bell*

It is certain that the noblest souls are the most extensively compassionate, for narrow and degenerate minds think that compassion belongs not to them; but a great soul, the noblest part of creation, is ever compassionate.

Bacon, Francis, 1561-1626 (English statesman), *Advancement of Learning*

When I was just a little girl, I would follow my father down the creaking, wooden stairs into the damp chamber of our family wine cellar. He would go down to kill the mice who lived there and I would go down to save them.

Bardot, Brigitte (French actress), April 1989

I believe if you can find it in your heart and mind to empathize with and respect nonhuman life, then I think your capacity, your *capability*, for love is that much greater. Joining this [animal protection] movement is like 'loving thy neighbor' in its highest sense.

Barnes, Donald, Ph.D. (Psychologist), June 1989

The day may come, when the rest of the animal creation may acquire those rights which never could have been withheld from them but by the hand of tyranny....It may come one day to be recognized, that the number of legs, the villosity of the skin, or the termination of the os sacrum, are reasons....insufficient for abandoning a sensitive being....What else is it that should trace the insuperable line? Is it the faculty of reason, or perhaps the faculty of discourse? But a full grown horse or dog is beyond comparison a more rational, as well as a more conversable animal, than an infant of a day, or a week, or even a month old. But suppose the case were otherwise, what would it avail? The question is not can they reason? Nor, can they talk? But can they suffer?

Bentham, Jeremy, 1748-1832 (English philosopher), *Principles of Morals and Legislation*

We need another and a wiser and perhaps a more mystical concept of animals. Remote from universal nature, and living by complicated artifice, man in civilization surveys the creature through the glass of his knowledge and sees thereby a feather magnified and the whole image in distortion. We patronize them for their incompleteness, for their tragic fate of having taken form so far below ourselves. And therein we err, and greatly err. For the animal shall not be measured by man. In a world older and more complete than ours they move finished and complete, gifted with extensions of the senses we have lost or never attained, living by voices we shall never hear. They are not brethren, they are not underlings; they are other nations, caught with ourselves in the net of life and time, fellow prisoners of the splendour and travail of the earth.

Beston, Henry, 1888-1968 (American naturalist author), *The Outermost House*, 1928

A righteous man has regard for the life of his beast, but the mercy of the wicked is cruel.

Bible, The, Proverbs 12:10

The Lord is good to all, and his compassion is over all that he has made.

Bible, The, Psalms 145:9

Life is life's greatest gift. Guard the life of another creature as you would your own because it is your own. On life's scale of values, the smallest is no less precious to the creature who owns it than the largest...

Biggle, Lloyd, Jr. (American author), *The Light That Never Was*, 1972

There are, I know, people who do not love animals, but I think this is because they do not understand them—or because, indeed, they do not really see them. For me, animals have always been a special part of the wonder of nature—the smallest as well as the largest—with their amazing variety, their beautifully contrived shapes and fascinating habits. I am captivated by the spirit of them. I find in them a longing to communicate and a real capacity for love. If sometimes they do not trust but fear man, it is because he has treated them with arrogance and insensitivity.

Casals, Pablo, 1876-1973 (Spanish-born cellist and conductor), quoted in *Peaceful Kingdom*, 1997

The love for all living creatures is the most noble attribute of man.

Darwin, Charles, 1809-1882 (British naturalist), *The Descent of Man*

Failure to recognize our responsibilities to the animal kingdom is the cause of many of the calamities which now beset the nations of the world....Nearly all of us have a deep rooted wish for peace—peace on earth; but we shall never attain the true peace—the peace of love, and not the uneasy equilibrium of fear—until we recognize the place of animals in the scheme of things and treat them accordingly.

Dowding, Lord, 1882-1970, House of Lords, July 18, 1957

Our individual worlds are only as wide as our empathy. Why identify with only one species when we can be so much larger? Animal encompasses human....When we finally cross the species boundary that keeps other animals oppressed, we will have crossed the boundary that circumscribes our lives.

Dunayer, Joan (Writer), in *Animals & Women*, 1995

Non-violence leads to the highest ethics, which is the goal of all evolution. Until we stop harming all other living beings, we are still savages.

Edison, Thomas A., 1847-1931 (American inventor), 1890

A human being is a part of the whole, called by us 'Universe,' a part limited in time and space. He experiences himself, his thoughts and feelings as something separated from the rest— a kind of optical delusion of his consciousness. This delusion is a kind of prison for us, restricting us to our personal desires and to affection for a few persons nearest to us. Our task must be to free ourselves from this prison by widening our circle of compassion to embrace all living creatures and the whole nature in its beauty.

Einstein, Dr. Albert, 1879-1955 (Nobel Prize-winning physicist), *New York Post*, November 28, 1972

Tenderness and pity should never be taken as weakness. Men who have been great in the true sense have never been indifferent to the rights, nor blind to the needs, of the helpless....Kindness toward all sentient creatures and compassion for suffering in all its forms are the hallmarks of the enlightened community and the badge of the cultural individual.

Farnum, George R., 1885-1973 (Assistant Attorney General of the United States), *Reverence for Life*

The ultimate expression of being fully human is to be open to the world within and without and to embrace all of life equally with reverence, humility and compassion....The missing link between animals and a truly humane mankind is man himself, who does not yet see himself as a part of the world, claiming it instead for himself.

Fox, Michael W., D.Sc., Ph.D., B.Vet. Med. (Ethologist), *One Earth, One Mind*, 1980

Not to hurt our humble brethren is our first duty to them, but to stop there is not enough. We have a higher mission—to be of service to them wherever they require it.

Francis of Assisi, Saint, 1181-1226, quoted in *Life* by St. Bonaventura

The greatness of a nation and its moral progress can be judged by the way its animals are treated.

Gandhi, Mohandas Karamchand, 1869-1948, The Mahatma (Great Soul), *The Moral Basis of Vegetarianism*

Compassion struggles, always. Indifference brushes it aside, selfish pursuit forces it on the defensive. When cruelty is given free rein, compassion becomes muted, even derided....As a religious person and minister, I believe the creatures belong to no one but God. We cannot own life. However, the quality of our relating to life determines our measure as human beings. The kingdom of God is the kingdom of right relationships.

Gist, Reverend Richard (Minister and writer), newspaper commentary, October 1998

I have known a large number of good souls who offered up the most sincere wishes for the establishment of this doctrine of humaneness, who thought it just and true in all its aspects, who believed in all that it announces; but who, in spite of so praiseworthy a disposition, dared not be the first to give the example. They awaited this movement from minds stronger than their own. Doubtless such are the minds which give the impulse to the world; but is it necessary to await this movement when one is convinced of one's self? Is it permissible to temporize in a question of agony and torture for innocent beings whose sole crime is to have been born?

Gleïzès, Jean Antoine, 1773-1843, *Thalysie: ou La Nouvelle Existence*

Nothing living should ever be treated with contempt. Whatever it is that lives, a man, a tree, or a bird, should be touched gently, because the time is short.

Goudge, Elizabeth, 1900-1984 (English author), *The Joy of the Snow*, 1974

[When asked about the difference between charitable causes for people and those for animals] I think they're the same thing. It's a feeling for life—all life.

Grace of Monaco, Princess, 1929-1982, quoted in *Peaceful Kingdom*, 1997

Kindness to all God's creatures is an absolute rock-bottom necessity if peace and righteousness are to prevail.

Grenfell, Sir Wilfred, 1865-1940 (English medical missionary), *The Adventure of Life*

Humaneness is, I believe, a reverence and respect for all life. It is not, finally, survival that we seek, but a quality of life that gives meaning and purpose to our existence. Yet, not for the sake of our life alone, but for the sake of all that lives.

Hoyt, John A. (President Emeritus, The Humane Society of the United States), *Humane Education: An Overview*

That which is good for one form of life enhances all. Protecting animals is enabling. Not doing so is demeaning not only to oneself but also to the interdependence of Creation, upon which survival depends.

Irwin, Paul G. (President, The Humane Society of the United States), 1992

The more we come in contact with animals and observe their

behavior, the more we love them, for we see how great is their care of their young.

Kant, Immanuel, 1724-1804 (German philosopher), *Lectures on Ethics*

Mankind's true moral test, its fundamental test (which lies deeply buried from view), consists of its attitude towards those who are at its mercy: animals. And in this respect mankind has suffered a fundamental debacle, a debacle so fundamental that all others stem from it.

Kundera, Milan (Author and critic), *The Unbearable Lightness of Being*, 1984

We owe it to ourselves and the animal world as well to create, not merely a body of rules and regulations to govern our conduct, but a level of sensibility that makes us care, deeply and constructively, about the entire planet and all of its varied inhabitants. If we can accomplish this, then perhaps, some far-off day, those who follow us down the track of the generations will be able to dwell in relative harmony with all of the creatures of the earth, human and non-human.

Kunstler, William, 1919-1995 (Attorney), March 1993

The moral unity to be expected in different ages is not a unity of standard, or of acts, but a unity of tendency....At one time the benevolent affections embrace merely the family, soon the circle expanding includes first a class, then a nation, then a coalition of nations, then all humanity, and finally, its influence is felt in the dealings of man with the animal world.

Lecky, W. E. H., 1838-1903 (Irish historian), *The History of European Morals*

I am in favour of animal rights as well as human rights. That is the way of a whole human being.

Lincoln, Abraham, 1809-1865 (16th President of the United States), *Complete Works*

Those who deny freedom to others deserve it not for themselves and under a just God cannot long retain it.

Lincoln, Abraham, 1809-1865 (16th President of the United States)

[Reply to friends who chided him for delaying them by stopping to return a fledgling to its nest] I could not have slept tonight if I had left that helpless little creature to perish on the ground.

Ibid

The fidelity of a dog is a precious gift demanding no less binding moral responsibilities than the friendship of a human being.

Lorenz, Konrad, 1903-1989 (Austrian zoologist), *Man Meets Dog*

Animals are, like us, endangered species on an endangered planet, and we are the ones who are endangering them, it, and ourselves. We owe them, at the very least, to refrain from harming them further. If no more, we could leave them be.

Masson, Jeffrey Moussaieff, Ph.D., *When Elephants Weep*, 1995

Why is compassion not part of our established curriculum, an inherent part of our education? Compassion, awe, wonder, curiosity, exaltation, humility—these are the very foundation of any real civilization, no longer the prerogatives, the preserves of any one church, but belonging to everyone, every child in every home, in every school.

Menuhin, Sir Yehudi (American-born virtuoso violinist), *Just for Animals*

The world stands greatly in need of men and women who are both compassionate and intelligent.

Montagu, Dr. Ashley (British-American anthropologist), *Growing Young*, 1981

As an anthropologist I have come to believe in the possibility of a universal humanity which takes the whole of animate and inanimate nature as its community, a humanity which is devoted to the encouragement of the childlike qualities with which all humans are endowed. It is in the education of those childlike traits, among them the love of animals, illumined by the inspiring knowledge we have accumulated in the world in which we live, that I see the most promising answer to the questions raised by the Conference.

Montagu, Dr. Ashley (British-American anthropologist), keynote address to the International Conference on Religious Perspectives on the Use of Animals in Science, London, July 25-27, 1984

It is necessary and urgent that following the example of the poor man (St. Francis) one decides to abandon inconsiderate forms of domination, capture and custody with respect to all creatures.

Paul, Pope John, II, quoted in *Animals and Christianity*, edited by Andrew Linzey and Tom Regan, 1990

So often when you start talking about kindness to animals...someone comments that starving and mistreated children should come first. The issue can't be divided like that. It isn't a choice between animals and children. It's our duty to care for both. Kindness is the important thing. Kids and animals are our responsibility.

Pearl, Minnie (Singer/entertainer), newspaper quote

[Imagine] that Steven Spielberg's E.T. and some of E.T.'s friends show up on Earth. Whatever else we may want to say of them, we do not want to say that they are members of our species, the species *Homo Sapiens*. Now, if a difference in species is a morally relevant difference, we should be willing to say that it is *not* wrong to kill or otherwise harm E.T. and the other members of his biological species in sport hunting, for example, even though it *is* wrong to do this to members of our species for this reason. But no double standards are allowed. If *their* belonging to a different species makes it all right for us to kill or harm them, then *our* belonging to a different species from the one to which they belong will cancel the wrongness of their killing or harming us. 'Sorry, chum,' E.T.'s compatriots say, before taking aim at us or prior to inducing *our* heart attacks, 'but you just don't belong to the right species.'

Regan, Dr. Tom (Professor of Philosophy, North Carolina State University), "Ill-gotten Gains," in *The Great Ape Project*, 1993

The capacity to suffer is the crucial similarity between men

souls like ourselves

and animals that binds us all together and places us all in a similar moral category.

Ryder, Dr. Richard (Clinical psychologist), *Victims of Science*, 1983

It is not THIS bloodshed or THAT bloodshed that must cease, but ALL bloodshed—all wanton infliction of pain or death.

Salt, Henry, 1851-1939 (English scholar and writer), *Seventy Years Among Savages*

Universal compassion is the only guarantee of morality.

Schopenhauer, Arthur, 1788-1860 (German philosopher), *On the Basis of Morality*

I must interpret the life about me as I interpret the life that is my own. My life is full of meaning to me. The life around me must be full of significance to itself. If I am to expect others to respect my life, then I must respect the other life I see, however strange it may be to mine. And not only other human life, but all kinds of life: life above mine, if there be such life; life below mine, as I know it to exist. Ethics in our Western world has hitherto been largely limited to the relations of man to man. But that is a limited ethics. We need a boundless ethics which will include the animals also.

Schweitzer, Albert, Ph.D., M.D., 1875-1965 (Nobel Peace Prize-winning humanitarian), *Civilization and Ethics*, 1949

A man is really ethical only when he obeys the constraint laid on him to aid all life which he is able to help, and when he goes out of his way to avoid injuring anything living. He does not ask how far this or that life deserves sympathy as valuable in itself, nor how far it is capable of feeling. To him life as such is sacred.

Ibid

The man who has become a thinking being feels a compulsion to give every will-to-live the same reverence for life that he gives his own. He experiences that other life in his own.

Ibid

The thinking man must oppose all cruel customs no matter how deeply rooted in tradition and surrounded by a halo.

Ibid

Until he extends the circle of his compassion to all living things, man will not himself find peace.

Schweitzer, Albert, Ph.D., M.D., 1875-1965 (Nobel Peace Prize-winning humanitarian), *The Philosophy of Civilization*, 1949

The worst sin towards our fellow creatures is not to hate them, but to be indifferent to them. That's the essence of inhumanity.

Shaw, George Bernard, 1856-1950 (Nobel Prize-winning author), *The Devil's Disciple*

If possessing a higher degree of intelligence does not entitle one human to use another for his own ends, how can it entitle humans to exploit nonhumans?

Singer, Peter, Ph.D. (Professor of Philosophy, Monash University, Australia), in *Animal Rights and Human Obligations*, 1976

Just as it is not possible to lay claim to a non-violent life while ignoring or co-operating with a militaristic or racist institution, neither is it possible to be genuinely non-violent while ignoring the violence done to the myriad varieties of life with which we share the planet.

Salamone, Connie, from *Reweaving the Web of Life*, ed. Pam McAllister, 1982

Nowadays we don't think much of a man's love for an animal; we laugh at people who are attached to cats. But if we stop loving animals, aren't we bound to stop loving humans too?

Solzhenitsyn, Alexander (Nobel Prize-winning Russian novelist), *Cancer Ward*, 1968

No humane being, past the thoughtless age of boyhood, will wantonly murder any creature which holds its life by the same tenure that he does.

Thoreau, Henry D., 1817-1862 (American poet and philosopher), *Walden*

The human-animal relationship is one of the cornerstones of a just and compassionate society. Beginning in childhood and continuing throughout life, the bonds we form with our companion animals can provide the basis of respect and regard for all living things.

Thornton, Gus W., D.V.M. (President, Massachusetts Society for the Prevention of Cruelty to Animals), 1999

The animals of the world exist for their own reasons. They were not made for humans any more than black people were made for whites or women for men....The pain felt by humans who are abused and the pain felt by non-human animals who are abused...[is] the same pain.

Walker, Alice (Pulitzer Prize-winning author), foreword, *The Dreaded Comparison* by Marjorie Spiegel, 1988

If we claim to love all of God's creatures, the criterion of that claim should be our willingness to work toward the alleviation of their agonies. If a being suffers, there can be no moral justification for disregarding that suffering.

Wyler, Gretchen (Actress and President, The Ark Trust), speech, 1980

souls like ourselves

*W*e find amongst animals, as amongst men, power of feeling pleasure, power of feeling pain; we see them moved by love and by hate; we see them feeling terror and attraction; we recognize in them powers of sensation closely akin to our own, and while we transcend them immensely in intellect, yet, in mere passional characteristics our natures and the animals' are closely allied. We know that when they feel terror, that terror means suffering. We know that when a wound is inflicted, that wound means pain to them. We know that threats bring to them suffering; they have a feeling of shrinking, of fear, of absence of friendly relations, and at once we begin to see that in our relations to the animal kingdom a duty arises which all thoughtful and compassionate minds should recognize—the duty that because we are stronger in mind than the animals, we are or ought to be their guardians and helpers, not their tyrants and oppressors, and we have no right to cause them suffering and terror merely for the gratification of the palate, merely for an added luxury to our own lives.

Besant, Annie, 1847-1933 (British social reformer), from a speech given in Manchester, England, October 1897

A Sacred Kinship I would not forgo binds me to all that breathes.

Boyeson, Hjalmar Hjorth, 1848-1895 (Norwegian-born writer)

In some far part of the Universe, ten thousand years from this noon, we may well confront creatures more vital, more intelligent than ourselves, who will read in our eyes, one hopes, a similar signal. What we want at that moment is recognition. Acceptance. A welcoming into some universal sill. And, once in, we would also hope, there is no killing club behind the door.

Bradbury, Ray (Science fiction author), August 1990

I personally can see no reason for conceding mind to my fellow men and denying it to animals...I at least cannot doubt that the interests and activities of animals are correlated with awareness and feeling in the same way as my own, and which may be, for ought I know, just as vivid.

Brain, Lord Walter Russell, 1895-1966 (Eminent British neurologist), from presidential address quoted Keele & Smith, *The Assessment of Pain in Men and Animals*

A cow who has been killed, skinned, dismembered and ground up or sliced is 'beef,' 'leather,' 'hind-quarter,' 'hamburger.' A laboratory rat is a 'research tool' or 'model.' A deer or a fox on a wildlife 'refuge' becomes a 'resource' deserving of 'conservation.' Using these words, it is hard, if not impossible, to understand non-human animals as creatures that, like ourselves, experience pain and suffering and have complicated emotional lives.

Carlsen, Spence (Philosopher) *Los Angeles Times,* April 22, 1987

If I learned anything from my time among the elephants, it is the extent to which we are kin. The warmth of their families makes me feel warm. Their capacity for delight gives me joy. Their ability to learn and understand things is a continuing revelation for me. If a person can't see these qualities when looking at elephants, it can only be because he or she doesn't want to.

Chadwick, Douglas (Wildlife biologist), *The Fate of the Elephant,* 1994

The Saints are exceedingly loving and gentle to mankind, and even to brute beasts....Surely we ought to show them [animals] great kindness and gentleness for many reasons, but, above all, because they are of the same origin as ourselves.

Chrysostom, Saint John, c. 347-407, *Homilies*

There are other sentient creatures all about us, who may lack our verbalizing gifts but who have their lives to live and their own visions of reality to worship. We are not separate from them, and owe them honour. To imagine that their lesser 'intelligence' (whatever that may be) licenses our tyranny is to leave the way open for any human intellectual elite to treat the rest of us as trash.

Clark, Stephen R. L. (Professor of Philosophy, Liverpool University, U.K.), *The Moral Status of Animals*, 1984

Life is as dear to a mute creature as it is to a man. Just as one wants happiness and fears pain, just as one wants to live and not to die, so do other creatures.

Dalai Lama of Tibet, His Holiness, The XIV (Tibetan religious leader and Nobel Prize Laureate), *The Vegetarian Way*, 1967

Not a single syllable can be said for the immortality of man that cannot be said for every other animal that ever roamed the plains and fields and woods.

Darrow, Clarence, 1857-1938 (American lawyer), *The Story of My Life*

There is no fundamental difference between man and the higher mammals in their mental faculties....The difference in mind between man and the higher animals, great as it is, certainly is one of degree and not of kind.

Darwin, Charles, 1809-1882 (British naturalist), *The Descent of Man*

One does not meet oneself until one catches the reflection from an eye other than human.

Eiseley, Loren, 1907-1977 (American environmental philosopher), *The Unexpected Universe*, 1969

From an evolutionary point of view, taking a chimpanzee's heart is like walking next door and ripping out my neighbor's heart. The chimpanzee is not as close to me as my daughter is, but we are related through a common ancestor. Like my neighbor, the chimpanzee is my cousin. If morality stops me from killing my human cousin, then it must also stop me from killing my chimpanzee cousin.

Fouts, Roger, Ph.D. (Professor of Psychology, Central Washington University), *Next of Kin: What Chimpanzees Have Taught Me About Who We Are*, 1997

If the biological sciences have taught us one thing over the last one hundred years, it is that drawing all-or-nothing lines between species is completely futile. Nature is a great continuum. With every passing year we discover more evidence to support Darwin's revolutionary hypothesis that the cognitive and emotional lives of animals differ only by degree, from the fishes to the birds to monkeys to humans.

Ibid

Kinship with all life must be expressed in *action* since belief is no longer enough. Above and beyond our own immediate needs we all have a responsibility as stewards of this small planet since we have a reflective consciousness unlike any other animal, so far as is known.

Fox, Michael W., D.Sc., Ph.D., B.Vet.Med. (Ethologist),
Between Animal and Man, 1986

I want to realize brotherhood or identity not merely with the beings called human, but I want to realize identity with all life, even with such things as crawl upon earth.

Gandhi, Mohandas Karamchand, 1869-1948, The Mahatma
(Great Soul), quoted in *Words of Gandhi*

Now, for a moment, let us imagine beings who, although they differ genetically from Homo Sapiens by about 1 percent and lack speech, nevertheless behave similarly to ourselves, can feel pain, share our emotions and have sophisticated intellectual abilities. Would we, today, condone the use of those beings as slaves? Tolerate their capture and export from Africa? Laugh at degrading performances, taught through cruelty, shown on our television screens? Turn a blind eye to their imprisonment, in tiny barren cells, often in solitary confinement, even though they had committed no crimes? Buy products tested on them at the cost of their mental or physical torture?...Those beings exist and we do condone their abuse. They are called chimpanzees.

Goodall, Jane, Ph.D. (Ethologist), "Chimpanzees—Bridging the
Gap," in *The Great Ape Project*, 1993

I believe there is an essential quality of being that is as common to animals as to the man-animal. To be sure, it is lacking the mystical, metaphysical appropriations surrounding man which have evolved from the historical philosophies and religions....Yet, it is entirely possible that the essence of animal being is just as important as that of man's and, in a non-religious sense, just as sacred.

Hoyt, John A. (President Emeritus, The Humane Society of the United States), speech, 1986

Because they are so closely akin to us and share our unknowingness, I loved all warm-blooded animals who have souls like ourselves and with whom, so I thought, we have an instinctive understanding. We experience joy and sorrow, love and hate, hunger and thirst, fear and trust in common — all the essential features of existence with the exception of speech, sharpened consciousness, and science. And although I admired science in the conventional way, I also saw it giving rise to alienation and aberration from God's world, as leading to a degeneration which animals were not capable of. Animals were dear and faithful, unchanging and trustworthy.

Jung, Dr. Carl G., 1875-1961 (Swiss-German psychoanalyst), "School Years," *Memories, Dreams, Reflections*, 1961

There is not a beast upon the earth, nor a bird that flies, but is a nation like to you.

Koran 6

Look into the eyes of an animal....And as you look into those eyes, reflect that this being is a never-to-be-duplicated expression of the universe....Pay attention to what you see: the years of living present within those eyes, and the vitality that shines through their color and transparency....Contemplate their shape. Notice the angles and curves of individuality that make the face of this creature a unique work of art, crafted by time and desire....And as you look into this being's eyes, pay attention also to what you cannot see, the inwardness, the selfhood, the 'I' that is as singular as its outward expression....What you look upon is a living spirit. Greet and respect it. Appreciate it for what it is....Ask yourself, what does it feel like to be this creature?...What does the world look like through its eyes?...Become aware of the great antiquity within those eyes—the millennia of evolution they hold within their gaze....Sense a solitude you can never fully enter into or understand....Be aware that this is a being who has known hardships and hurts you can never imagine. This is a being who has known moments of wildness and innocence that you can never share....Yet this is a creature who is alive and has desires like you. It walks the same ground and breathes the same air. It feels pain and enjoys its senses— the dazzling warmth of the sun, the cooling shade of the forests, the refreshing taste of pure water—as you do. And in this we are all kin....In that kinship, all life exists. Through that kinship we can find wholeness. Out of that kinship we can draw wisdom and understanding for the healing of our common home.

Kowalski, Gary (Unitarian Universalist minister), *The Souls of Animals*, 1991

Animals may differ in degree but not radically in kind from us. We demean ourselves by ignoring the evidence of our similarities and continuing with our prejudices against the rest of the animal kingdom.

Langley, Gill, Ph.D., Cambridge University Debate, October 1987

Many a time by the gods' comely shrines the calf falls in death, murdered close by the altars smoking with incense, while the blood's warm tide wells up from the heart. The mother, bereft of her offspring, wanders through the green glades; on the ground she sees its cloven hoofprints; she haunts every spot if perchance she might gain sight of her lost young one; she goes apart and utters her complaint to the leafy wood, and payeth many a visit to the stall, full of longing for her child. Nor tender willows, nor dew besprent grass, not the streams that glide between their deep banks, can avail to give her joy or shake off the load of care, nor can the sight of the other calves scattered o'er the joyous pasture, suffice to turn her thoughts aside, or lighten her of her care.

Lucretius, c. 99-55 B.C. (Latin poet and philosopher), *De Rerum Naturae*

There is no difference between the worry of a human mother and an animal mother for their offspring. A mother's love does not derive from the intellect but from the emotions, in animals just as in humans.

Maimonides, 1135-1204 (Rabbi of Cairo), *Guide for the Perplexed*

The point is that a goose or other animal may be a quivering mass of emotion. Its feelings may be 'written all over its face,' and only by ignorance, lack of interest, desire for exploitation (like wanting to eat them), or by anthropocentric prejudices that preclude us, as if by divine fiat, from recognizing commonality where it might exist.

Masson, Jeffrey Moussaieff, Ph.D., *When Elephants Weep*, 1995

The fact that some people are silly about animals cannot stop the topic being a serious one. Animals are not just one of the things with which people amuse themselves, like chewing-gum and water-skis, *they are the group to which people belong*. We are not just rather like animals; we *are* animals.

Midgley, Mary (Former Senior Lecturer in Philosophy, University of Newcastle-upon-Tyne, U.K.), *Philosophy* 48 (1973): 111-35

Orphan monkeys...are often adopted by the tribe and carefully looked after by the other monkeys, both male and female. The great mass of human beings, who know about as much about the real emotional life of monkeys as wooden Indians do, are inclined to pass over lightly all displays of feeling by these people of the trees. But the poet knows, and the prophet knows, and the world will one day understand, that in the gentle bosoms of these wild woodland mothers glow the antecedents of the same impulses as those that cast that blessed radiance over the lost paradise of our own sweet childhood. The mother monkey who gathered green leaves as she fled from limb to limb, and frantically stuffed them into the wound of her dying baby in order to staunch the cruel rush of blood from its side, all the while uttering the most pitiful cries and casting reproachful glances at her human enemy, until she fell with her darling in her arms and a bullet in her heart, had in her simian soul just as genuine motherlove, and love just as sacred, as that which burns in the breast of a woman.

Moore, J. Howard, 1862-1916 (Zoologist), *The Universal Kinship*, 1906

souls like ourselves

Animals share with us the privilege of having a soul.

Pythagoras, c. 570-500 B.C. (Greek philosopher and
mathematician)

There is always something adorable to me about a newborn
fawn, or a freshly-hatched duckling, or a newborn calf, or, in
fact, a newborn animal of any kind, including human new-
borns. They shine, there is a lustre about them, a shimmering
statement of the freshness they bring to life. To me, the fact
that newborn human infants and newborn animal babies of
all kinds glow with this ineffable sweetness testifies to our
common source. They are born as we are — fresh from the lap
of God, wanting to express their qualities in the service of the
divine spark within them. They are born, as we are, thirsting
for life. They are born, as we are, wanting to be all they are,
and become all they can become.

Robbins, John (Author), *Diet for a New America*, 1987

Surely if we are all God's creatures, if all animal species are
capable of feeling, if we are all evolutionary relatives, if all
animals are on the same biological continuum, then also we
should all be on the same moral continuum — and if it is
wrong to inflict suffering upon an innocent and unwilling
human, then it is wrong to so treat another species.

Ryder, Dr. Richard D. (Clinical psychologist), *Speciesism: The
Ethics of Animal Abuse*, 1970

If chimpanzees have consciousness, do they not have what
until now has been described as 'human rights'? How smart
does a chimpanzee have to be before killing him constitutes
murder?

Sagan, Dr. Carl, 1934-1996 (U.S. astronomer), *The Dragons of
Eden*, 1977

In spite of their boasted progress in sciences and arts, my
countrymen are still practically ignorant of the real kinship
which exists between mankind and the other races, and of the
duties which this kinship implies. They are still the victims of
that old anthropocentric superstition which pictures man as
the centre of the universe, and separated from the inferior
animals — mere playthings made for his august pleasure and

amusement—by a deep intervening gulf.

Salt, Henry, 1851-1939 (English scholar and writer), *Seventy Years Among Savages*

Next time you go to the beach or the park, take a look around and see who is happiest and enjoying the day to the fullest. Is it the intellectually sophisticated human adults, or is it the children and the dogs?...Consequently, if we recognize that all beings with feelings should be liberated from human exploitation precisely because they are feeling beings, we will have overcome speciesism and freed our morality from anthropocentric prejudice.

Sapontzis, Steve F. (Professor of Philosophy, California State University), "Aping Persons—Pro and Con," in *The Great Ape Project*, 1993

And what, I wonder, was going through the minds of a herd of elephants in Uganda who stood outside the store that housed the feet of hundreds of their cropped companions, and shoveled earth into it through a narrow opening until the feet were partially covered with soil? Why, I wonder, do elephants often cover bodies, with bush and grass, bodies not only of other elephants, but of other animals as well?...Who can say that animals are not capable of the same emotions and feelings as we ourselves?

Sheldrick, Daphne, M.B.E. (Wildlife rehabilitator, Nairobi, Kenya), *The Tsavo Story*

I once had a sparrow alight on my shoulder for a moment while I was hoeing in a village garden, and I felt that I was more distinguished by that circumstance than I should have been by any epaulet I could have worn.

Thoreau, Henry D., 1817-1862 (American poet and philosopher), *Walden*

souls like ourselves

3. RELIGION, SPIRITUALITY AND ANIMALS

I f we understand and feel that the greatest act of devotion and worship to God is not to hurt or harm any of His beings, we are loving God.

Baba, Meher, 1894-1969 (Spiritual master in western India), *The Theme of Creation and Its Purposes*

Christians, then, who close their minds and hearts to the cause of animal welfare and the evils it seeks to combat are ignoring the fundamental spiritual teaching of Christ himself....You in the animal welfare movement are among those who may yet save our society from becoming spiritually deaf, blind and dead, and so from the doom that will justly follow....

Baker, Reverend John Austin (Bishop of Salisbury [England]), sermon in Salisbury Cathedral, October 4, 1986

As many of the experiencers [of near-death and mystical experiences] I spoke with told me, the gift of human existence entails tremendous responsibility for God's creation because we live in partnership with the universe; we belong to God just as surely as God belongs to us....For those who truly revere God's creation, it quickly becomes obvious that anything that preserves and enhances life is essentially good, while anything that destroys, diminishes, or demeans life is bad.

Berman, Phillip (Theologian and author), *The Journey Home*, 1996

Ask the animals and they will teach you, or the birds of the air and they will tell you; or speak to the earth and it will teach you, and the fish of the sea will declare to you: Which of all these does not know that the hand of the Lord has done all this? In His hand is the soul of every living creature and the breath of all mankind.

Bible, The, Job 12:7-10

For the fate of the sons of men and the fate of beasts is the same; as one dies, so dies the other. They all have the same breath, and man has no advantage over the beasts; for all is vanity.

Bible, The, Ecclesiastes 3:19-21

Open your eyes, alert the ears of your spirit, open your lips and apply your heart so that in all creatures you may see, hear, praise, love and worship, glorify and honor your God.

Bonaventure, Saint, B.C. 1217-1274 (Medieval theologian)

He who, seeking his own happiness, punishes or kills beings who also long for happiness, will not find happiness after death.

Buddhism, *Dhammapada*

Because he has pity on every living creature, therefore is a man called 'holy.'

Ibid

One act of pure love in saving life is greater than spending the whole of one's time in religious offerings to the gods....

Ibid

For the sake of love of purity, the Bodhisattva [person who has achieved great moral and spiritual wisdom] should refrain from eating flesh....

Buddhism, *Lankavatara*

All beings seek for happiness; so let your compassion extend itself to all.

Buddhism, *Mahavamsa*

Unless you can so control your minds that even the thought

of brutal unkindness and killing is abhorrent, you will never be able to escape from the bondage of the world's life....

Buddhism, *Surangama*

When the center of the heart is touched, and a sense of compassion awakens with another person or creature, and you realize that you and that other are in some sense creatures of the one life in being, a whole new state of life in the spirit opens up.

Campbell, Joseph, 1904-1987 (American scholar/teacher/writer), *The Inner Reaches of Outer Space*, 1986

I have said it again and again, and I will say it on the day I die if I have time. It is wrong to cause pain. It is wrong to cause fear, and to allow preventable pain and preventable fear to exist is no less an offense than causing them....I am more sure of that than I am of my private view of God and religion. I am more sure of that than I am of anything else in my experience as a man. I believe that credo is a valid view of my responsibility on earth.

Caras, Roger (President, American Society for the Prevention of Cruelty to Animals) *The Fifth Day*

I saw deep in the eyes of the animals the human soul look out upon me. I saw where it was born deep down under feathers and fur, or condemned for awhile to roam fourfooted among the brambles. I caught the clinging mute glance of the prisoner, and swore that I would be faithful. Thee my brother and sister I see and mistake not. Do not be afraid. Dwelling thus and thus for a while, fulfilling thy appointed time—thou shalt come to thyself at last....Come nigh little bird with your half-stretched quivering wings—within you I behold choirs of angels, and the Lord himself in vista.

Carpenter, Edward, 1844-1929 (English social reform writer), *Towards Democracy*

Love all God's creation, the whole of it and every grain of sand. Love every leaf, every ray of God's light! Love the animals, love the plants, love everything. If you love everything, you will perceive the divine mystery in things. And once you have perceived it, you will begin to comprehend it ceaselessly more and more every day. And you will at last come to love the whole world with an abiding, universal love. Love the animals: God has given them the rudiments of thought and untroubled joy. Do not, therefore, trouble it, do not torture them, do not deprive them of their joy, do not go against God's intent.

Dostoevsky, Fyodor Mikhail, 1821-1881 (Russian novelist),
The Brothers Karamazov

It is the supreme task for humanity to fulfill itself without denying fulfillment to others, be they human or nonhuman beings.

Fox, Michael W., D.Sc., Ph.D., B.Vet.Med. (Ethologist),
St. Francis of Assisi, Animals, and Nature, 1989

It is man who has fallen, not the beasts: that is the message even for the irreligious, and to some extent salvation can be measured by his very treatment of them.

Fuller, Roy, 1912-1991 (British poet and novelist), *Fellow Mortals*

The concept known as *bal tashchit* — 'Do not destroy' — has a special significance in Jewish tradition....We are constantly being warned in our faith that the capricious, thoughtless, wasteful destruction of the elements and creatures of the earth is wrong....We should remind ourselves daily of our responsibility to all aspects of creation.

Geffen, David, M.D. (Oncologist), *Atlanta Jewish Times*,
February 1, 1980

Because he cannot really sense his own soul, the mundane religionist cannot sense it in other creatures and so thinks nothing of feasting on their slaughtered remains. Insisting that some living creatures have life but no soul, he inadvertently assumes the ideologic posture of the materialist, who reduces life to a mere biologic function. Under the sway of this contradiction, he fondles one lesser creature and slaughters another, pampering one as his pet and cannibalizing the other as his dinner. Devoid of even rudimentary consciousness of spirit, he remains blissfully unaware of his sin....His scriptures enjoin 'Thou shalt not kill,' but he kills with blind, grinding routine. 'As you did it to one of the least of these my brethren,' says Jesus, 'you did it to me.'

Gelberg, Steven J., *The Transcendental Imperative: The Case for "Otherworldly" Religion*, presented at Assembly of the World's Religions I, 1985

Anyone looking into the soulful eyes of a dog should be in no doubt that if a human has one, then other animals cannot be placed as soulless.

Grigg, John Edward Poynder, April 1962

When I was young I often heard quoted a piece of Christian philosophy which was taken as self-evidently true. It was the proposition that animals have no rights. This, of course, is true only in one sense. They are not human persons and therefore they have no rights, so to speak, in their own right. But they have very positive rights because they are God's creatures. If we have to speak with absolute accuracy we must say that God has the right to have all his creatures treated with proper respect.

Heenan, Cardinal, 1905-1975, foreword to *God's Animals*

Do not kill any animal for pleasure, see harmony in nature, and lend a helping hand to all living creatures.

Hindu proverb

Those who have forsaken the killing of all; those who are helpmates to all; those who are a sanctuary to all; those men are in the way of heaven.

Hinduism, *Hitopadesa*

What is religion? Compassion for all things which have life.

Ibid

We bow to all beings with great reverence in the thought and knowledge that God enters into them through fractioning Himself as living creatures.

Hinduism, *Mahabharata*

Non-injury, truthfulness, freedom from theft, lust, anger and greed, and an effort to do what is agreeable and beneficial to all creatures—this is the common duty of all castes.

Hinduism, *Srimad-Bhagavatam*

He who permits the slaughter of an animal, he who kills it, he who cuts it up, he who buys or sells meat, he who cooks it, he who serves it up and he who eats it, are all slayers....There is no greater sinner than that man who seeks to increase the bulk of his own flesh by the flesh of other beings.

Hinduism, *The Laws of Manu V, 45-52*

It becomes abundantly clear that man's cruelty to the creatures is largely due to his failure to realize who they are. That the creatures are not things should be obvious to the lowest intelligence. They are highly sensitive organisms—organisms capable of intense feeling and affection, and what is more, they are (like ourselves) creatures, i.e. creatures of our Heavenly Father....If we consider the testimony of those who have tried to understand them from a higher standpoint than the merely scientific one, we shall find that they all agree that they have souls and that these survive physical death. If it is objected that it is impossible to prove this, we would reply that it is equally difficult to prove that human beings have immortal souls. And yet in each case we can point to things which support such a belief. Just as there are desires implanted by God in man that can only be satisfied in a future existence, so there are traits in the character of the creatures which by their very nature must be eternal. Thus the self-sacrificing love and trust that a dog has for its master and the sorrow that it feels over the loss of a friend are qualities that are not only human, but divine.

Holmes-Gore, Reverend V. A., 1909-1952, *These We Have Not Loved*

Thou shalt love the stars, the ocean, the forest, and reverence all living things, recognizing that the source of life is one.

Hubbard, Elbert, 1856-1915 (American editor, publisher and author), *NoteBook of Elbert Hubbard*

Life is one, said the Buddha, and the Middle Way to the end of suffering in all its forms is that which leads to the end of the illusion of separation, which enables man to see, as a fact as clear as sunlight, that all mankind, and all other forms in manifestation, are one unit, the infinitely variable appearance of an indivisible Whole.

Humphreys, Christmas, 1901-1983 (Writer), *The Buddhist Way of Life*, 1969

The bottom line is that there can be no 'humane' procedure when slaughter is involved, nor can factory farming ever be made merciful. Ironically, the dilemma of Jewish ritual slaughter could be resolved by switching to a vegan diet, the grain-based diet set forth in Genesis.

Jacobs, Rabbi Sidney J., 1989

Harmlessness is the only religion.

Jainism, maxim

All breathing, existing, living, sentient creatures should not be slain nor treated with violence, nor abused, nor tormented, nor driven away. This is the pure unchangeable Law.

Jainism, *Sutrakritanga*

Ahimsa-paramo-dharmah—non-injury to living beings is the highest religion....In happiness and suffering, in joy and grief, we should regard all creatures as we regard our own self, and should therefore refrain from inflicting upon others such injury as would appear undesirable to us if inflicted upon ourselves.

Jainism, *Yogashastra*

I tremble for my species when I reflect that God is just.

Jefferson, Thomas, 1743-1790 (3rd President of the United States)

Moral and legal rules concerning the treatment of animals are based on the principle that animals are part of God's creation toward which man bears responsibility. Laws and other indications in the Pentateuch [the first five books of the Bible] and the rest of the Bible make it clear not only that cruelty to animals is forbidden but also that compassion and mercy to them are demanded of man by God.

Jewish Encyclopedia

souls like ourselves

3. RELIGION, SPIRITUALITY AND ANIMALS

And if thy heart be straight with God, then every creature shall be to thee a mirror of life and a book of holy doctrine, for there is no creature so little or so vile, but that sheweth and representeth the goodness of God.

Kempis, Thomas, 1379-1471 (German priest, monk and writer), *Imitation of Christ*

Every religion has taught that man should put himself on the side of the will of God in the world, on the side of good as against evil, of evolution as against retrogression. The man who ranges himself on the side of evolution realizes the wickedness of destroying life; for he knows that, just as he is here in this physical body in order that he may learn the lessons of this plane, so is the animal occupying his body for the same reason...He knows that the life behind the animal is the Divine Life, that all life in the world is Divine; the animals therefore are truly our brothers,...and we can have no sort of right to take their lives for the gratification of our perverted tastes—no right to cause them untold agony and suffering merely to satisfy our degraded and detestable lusts....We have brought these things to such a pass with our mis-called 'sport' and our wholesale slaughtering, that all wild creatures fly from the sight of us. Does that seem like the universal brotherhood of God's creatures?...There is an influence flowing back upon us from all this—an effect which you can hardly realize unless you are able to see how it looks when regarded with the sight of the higher plane. Every one of these creatures which you so ruthlessly murder in this way has its own thoughts and feelings with regard to all this; it has horror, pain and indignation, and an intense but unexpressed feeling of the hideous injustice of it all.

Leadbeater, Charles W., 1854-1934 (Renowned theosophist), *Vegetarianism and Occultism*

I care not much for a man's religion whose dog and cat are not the better for it.

Lincoln, Abraham, 1809-1865 (16th President of the United States), *Complete Works*

The creation waits with eager longing for the revealing of the

40

sons of God. And who are these? They are, simply put, Spirit-led individuals who will make possible a new order of existence; who will show by their life the possibility of newness of life.

Linzey, Reverend Dr. Andrew, Center for the Study of Theology, University of Essex, U.K., *Christianity and the Rights of Animals*, 1987

The point to be grasped from the saintly tradition is that to love animals is not sentimentality (as we know it) but true spirituality. Of course there can be vain, self-seeking loving, but to go (sometimes literally) out of our way to help animals, to expend effort to secure their protection and to feel with them their suffering and to be moved by it—these are surely signs of spiritual greatness.

Ibid

I do not see the theological basis on which we can go on saying that the human species is of such overwhelming, unique and colossal significance that it justifies, as a matter of course, the institutional exploitation of billions of other animals....None of us are pure as far as animal exploitation is concerned. Nevertheless, we need to hold before ourselves the vision of the peaceable kingdom. We should want a world in which there will be no injury, no suffering, no wanton killing. To this end we all need to be engaged in a program of progressive disengagement from injury to animals.

Linzey, Reverend Dr. Andrew, Center for the Study of Theology, University of Essex, U.K., April 1992

How can I teach your children gentleness and mercy to the weak and reverence for life, which in its nakedness and excess, is still a gleam of God's omnipotence, when by your laws, your action and your speech, you contradict the very things I teach?

Longfellow, Henry Wadsworth, 1807-1882 (American poet), *Letters*

It should not be believed that all beings exist for the sake of the existence of man. On the contrary, all the other beings too have been intended for their own sakes and not for the sake of anything else.

Maimonides, 1135-1204 (Rabbi of Cairo), *Guide for the Perplexed*

[Describing the outcome of a mystical experience] Since the revelations, everywhere I look I see myself. There I go: that bald man, this angry child, that fearful cat, that cool stone, that bubbling brook, that worm struggling for its life, that bird desperate to feed her hungry babies, that one trapped in his rage, this one anxious but fearful of finding out why. Hardly strangers! Empathy is the life of the soul, I think, because the soul that allows us to see the one in the other is the soul that finds joy.

Michele, Claudia (Psychotherapist), quoted in *The Journey Home* by Phillip Berman, 1996

Never think of anyone as inferior to you. Open the inner Eye and you will see the One Glory shining in all creatures.

Misri, 9th century (Sufi saint), quoted in *Meditations of the Masters*, Ellen Kei Hua, ed.

There is not an animal on earth, nor a bird that flies on its wings, but they are communities like you.

Mohammed, 570-632

All beings are *ends*; no creatures are *means*. All beings have not equal rights, neither have all men; but *all have rights*. The *Life Process* is the *End—not man*, nor any other animal temporarily privileged to weave a world's philosophy. Non-human beings were not made for human beings any more than human beings were made for non-human beings....The great Law, the all inclusive gospel of social salvation, is to act toward others as you would act toward a part of your own self.

Moore, J. Howard, 1862-1916 (Zoologist), *The Universal Kinship*, 1906

We don't own animals, any more than we don't own trees or own mountains or seas or, indeed, each other. We don't own our wives or our husbands or our friends or our lovers. We respect and behold and we celebrate trees and mountains and seas and husbands and wives and lovers and children and friends and animals.

Morton, Reverend James, Cathedral of St. John the Divine, New York City, sermon, 1986

Thus godlike sympathy grows and thrives and spreads far beyond the teachings of churches and schools, where too often the mean, blinding, loveless doctrine is taught that animals have neither mind nor soul, have not rights that we are bound to respect, and were made only for man, to be petted, spoiled, slaughtered, or enslaved.

Muir, John, 1838-1914 (Scottish-American naturalist), *The Story of My Boyhood*

The moral duty of man consists of imitating the moral goodness and beneficence of God manifested in the creation toward all his living creatures. Everything of persecution and revenge between man and man, and everything of cruelty to animals, is a violation of moral duty.

Paine, Thomas, 1737-1809 (English-American writer), *The Age of Reason*

Nor can the moral character of development exclude respect for the beings which constitute the natural world, which the ancient Greeks—alluding precisely to the order which distinguishes it—called the 'cosmos.' Such realities also demand respect, by virtue of a threefold consideration which it is useful to reflect upon carefully....The first consideration is the appropriateness of acquiring a growing awareness of the fact that one cannot use with impunity the different categories of beings, whether living or inanimate—animals, plants, the natural elements—simply as one wishes, according to one's own economic needs. On the contrary, one must take into account the nature of each being and of its mutual connection in an ordered system which is precisely the 'cosmos.'

Paul, Pope John, II, *On Social Concerns*, December 30, 1987, paragraph 34

Has God, thou fool, worked solely for thy good, thy joy, thy pastime, thy attire, thy food? Who for thy table feeds the wanton fawn, for him as kindly spread the flowr'y lawn: Is it for thee the lark ascends and sings? Joy tunes his voice, joy

souls like ourselves

elevates his wings: Is it for thee the linnet pours his throat? Loves of his own and raptures swell the note....Know, Nature's children all divide her care; the fur that warms a monarch warm'd a bear. While man exclaims, 'See all things for my use!' 'See man for mine!' replies a pampered goose; and just as short of reason must he fall, who thinks all made for one, not one for all.

Pope, Alexander, 1688-1744 (English poet), *Essay on Man*

All that breathes is precious. Who is to say that the suffering of a sparrow is less worthy of solace than the pain of a man? The spark of life is no dimmer simply because it is encased in fur or feather.

Punshi, Dr. R. K. (Veterinarian, Charity Birds Hospital, Delhi, India), 1986

There is nothing in the Bible that would justify our modern-day policies and programs that despoil the land, desecrate the environment, and destroy entire species of wildlife. Such actions clearly violate God's commands to humans to 'replenish the earth,' conserve natural resources, and treat animals with kindness....

Regenstein, Lewis G. (Director of the Interfaith Council for the Protection of Animals and Nature), introduction, *Replenish the Earth*, 1991

Animal advocates do what they do because, whether conscious of it or not, they are trying to respond to a divine ethic. Working with justice and compassion for the good of suffering creation, they must sooner or later recognize that improving man's relations to animals is but a reflection of man's closer relation to deity.

Roberts, Dr. Catherine (Microbiologist), *Spectrum Review*, No. 3, Spring 1988

[Describing a near-death experience] Anyone who has had such an experience of God, who has felt such a profound sense of connection with reality, knows that there is only one truly significant work to do in life, and that is to love; to love nature, to love people, to love animals, to love creation itself, just because it is. To serve God's creation with a warm and loving hand of generosity and compassion—that is the only meaningful existence.

Rodonaia, George, M.D., Ph.D., quoted in *The Journey Home* by Phillip Berman, 1996

I know of no more beautiful prayer than that which the Hindus of old used in closing their public spectacles. It was: 'May all that have life be delivered from suffering!'

Schopenhauer, Arthur, 1788-1860 (German philosopher), *On the Basis of Morality*

Boundless compassion for all living things is the surest and most certain guarantee of pure moral conduct, and needs no casuistry. Whoever is filled with it will assuredly injure no one, encroach on no man's rights; he will rather have regard for every one, forgive every one, help every one as far as he can, and all his actions will bear the stamp of justice and loving-kindness.

Ibid

If I have an animal—be it only a calf or a hen—a living, sensitive creature, am I allowed to treat it as nothing but a utility? Am I allowed to run it to ruin?...It is no use trying to answer such questions scientifically. They are metaphysical, not scientific questions. It is a metaphysical error, likely to produce the gravest, practical consequences, to equate 'car' and 'animal' on account of their utility, while failing to recognize the most fundamental difference between them, that of 'level of being.'

Schumacher, Dr. E. F., 1911-1977 (English economist and philosopher), *Small is Beautiful*, 1973

Any religion or philosophy which is not based on a respect for life is not a true religion or philosophy.

Schweitzer, Albert, Ph.D., M.D., 1875-1965 (Nobel Peace Prize-winning humanitarian), letter, 1961

There is no religion without love, and people may talk as much as they like about their religion, but if it does not teach them to be good and kind to beasts as well as man it is all a sham.

Sewell, Anna, 1820-1878 (British author), *Black Beauty*

This sense of the kinship of all forms of life is all that is needed to make Evolution not only a conceivable theory, but an inspiring one. St. Anthony was ripe for the Evolution theory when he preached to the fishes, and St. Francis when he called the birds his little brothers. Our vanity, and our snobbish conception of Godhead as being, like earthly kingship, a supreme class distinction instead of the rock on which Equality is built, has led us to insist on God offering us special terms by placing us apart from and above all the rest of his creatures.

Shaw, George Bernard, 1856-1950 (Nobel Prize-winning author), *The Sunday Express*, August 1927

You think those dogs will not be in Heaven! I tell you they will be there long before any of us.

Stevenson, Robert Louis, 1850-1894 (Scottish author), *Familiar Studies of Men and Books*

If man aspires towards a righteous life, his first act of abstinence is from injury to animals.

Tolstoy, Leo Nikolayevich, 1828-1910 (Russian novelist), *The First Step*

The Golden Rule must be applied in our relations with the animal world, just as it must be applied in our relations with our fellow men, and no one can be a Christian until this finds embodiment in his or her life.

Trine, Ralph Waldo, 1866-1958 (Writer), *Every Living Creature*

The animals of the planet are in desperate peril...Without free animal life I believe we will lose the spiritual equivalent of oxygen.

Walker, Alice (Pulitzer Prize-winning author), *Living by the Word*, 1988

The Golden Rule is a natural consequence of the recognition of the unity of being. The sufferings of other living creatures then evoke the tenderness and care that we should wish for ourselves in like circumstances, and a determination to do nothing that will add to the general misery of sentient life, but instead to live harmlessly and lovingly as expressions of the

God towards which things are so painfully striving.
Wynne-Tyson, Esme, 1898-1972 (English actress and writer),
The Philosophy of Compassion

souls like ourselves

4. ANIMAL CONSUMPTION AND VEGETARIANISM

*V*egetable diet and sweet repose. Animal food and nightmare. Pluck your body from the orchard; do not snatch it from the shambles. Without flesh diet there could be no bloodshedding war.

Alcott, Louisa May, 1832-1888 (Author and social reformer),
Life, Letters and Journals

With sober living, well being increases in the household, animals are in safety, there is no shedding of blood, nor putting animals to death.

Basil, Saint, 329-379 (Bishop of Caesarea)

Of course it would *not* be good for business if too many people realized that milk is not essential to optimum health. Coupled with some of the disadvantages of relying on this product of the over-worked, sex-hormoned, antibiotic-filled, semi-invalid cow, with her proneness to udder complaints, umbilical sepsis, mastitis and chronic catarrh, etc., it might well bring about a new and refreshing outlook on food habits.

Batt, Eva V. (British author), *World Forum*, October 1961

Vegetarianism is not a fad. It is a great and essential part of the religion of humanity. It is a step into a higher, because a less selfish, plane of life. It makes progress possible, and both individual and social development is at present seriously blocked by the meat habit and all that it implies and involves....As long as we treat other living, sensitive creatures with like feelings as ours only as carcasses for the market and meat to be consumed, we must shut our eyes to the real kinship of all living things, and thus lose an essential factor in learning to understand, even in some degree, this mysterious world in which we find ourselves.

Bell, Ernest, 1851-1933 (British publisher and humanitarian), *Summer School Papers*

We cannot by any stretch of amiability say, or feel, that the meat-eater is actuated by any lofty motive in his choice. He has no unselfish ideal to work out in the matter. His whole effort is to defend or excuse that which his *feelings* all the time tell him is a selfish and cruel practice. He has to shut his eyes to much that he dares not face, to try to invent, so-called scientific reasons to excuse that which in itself is obviously very undesirable and discreditable—'a painful necessity,' as he sometimes calls it.

Ibid

Vegetarianism is a way of life that we should all move toward for economic survival, physical well-being, and spiritual integrity.

Berry, Father Thomas (Catholic priest and writer), in *Food for the Spirit*

Let us then pursue what makes for peace and for mutual upbuilding. Do not, for the sake of food, destroy the work of God. Everything is indeed clean, but it is wrong for any one to make others fall by what he eats; it is right not to eat meat or drink wine or do anything that makes your brother stumble.

Bible, The, Romans 14:19-20

I don't myself believe that, even when we fulfill our minimum obligations not to cause pain, we have the right to kill animals. I know I would not have the right to kill you, however painlessly, just because I liked your flavour, and I am not in a position to judge that your life is worth more to you than the animals' to it.

Brophy, Brigid, 1929-1995 (British novelist), *Don't Never Forget*

To us, the thought of burning a woman alive in public is a horrible abomination, but it was practiced as a social necessity in the Middle Ages. A few hundred years from now, our descendants will not be able to recall our habit of raising friendly animals in order to kill them and eat their decaying bodies without repulsion.

Byrom, Michael (English author), *Evolution for Beginners*

Our study [China Diet and Health Study] suggests that the closer one approaches a total plant food diet, the greater the health benefit....It turns out that animal protein, when consumed, exhibits a variety of undesirable health effects. Whether it is the immune system, various enzyme systems, the uptake of carcinogens into the cells, or hormonal activities, animal protein generally only causes mischief. High fat intake still can be a problem, and we ought not to be consuming such high-fat diets. But I suggest that animal protein is more problematic in this whole diet/disease relationship than is total fat.

Campbell, Colin, M.S., Ph.D. (Professor of Nutritional Biochemistry, Cornell University), interview, 1994

I cannot find any great difference, on the foot of natural reason and equity only, between feeding on human flesh and feeding on [other] animal flesh, except custom and example.

Cheyne, George, 1671-1743 (English author and physician), *Essay on Regimen*

[Meat diet] is inimical to the upward evolutionary ascent of the human nature.

Chidananda, Swami, XXIV World Vegetarian Congress, 1977

I do not see any reason why animals should be slaughtered to serve as human diet when there are so many substitutes. After all, man can live without meat. It is only some carnivorous animals that have to subsist on flesh. Killing animals for sport, for pleasure, for adventures, and for hides and furs is a phenomenon which is at once disgusting and distressing. There is no justification in indulging in such acts of brutality.

Dalai Lama of Tibet, His Holiness, The XIV (Tibetan religious leader and Nobel Prize Laureate), 1967

Why is it that kindly persons, people endowed with pity and compassion, folk of quick sympathy who have tears for the lightest ailment of their pet cat or dog, can endure this daily rottenness, this daily massacre, this sacrifice the voices of whose victims rise up to heaven in wearisome lament, in an unending stream of despairing appeal? The outstanding reasons are an utter dearth of imagination and the terrific power of habit. There is not a single person present who would or could be so heartless, or so bloodthirsty, or so barbarous as to go out and prepare a dinner by taking a lamb frolicking in the field, 'the lamb that looks you in the face,' as Shelley said, and kill it.

Davis, Reverend J. T., 1872-1944, quoted in *It is the Privilege of Power to Protect*

Man alone consumes and engulfs more flesh than all other animals put together. He is, then, the greatest destroyer, and he is so more by abuse than by necessity.

De Buffon, George Louis Leclerc, 1707-1788 (French naturalist), *L'Histoire Naturelle*

If animals experience not only pain, but also the desire to avoid pain, why does the meat-eater feel justified in causing them unnecessary pain? Rather than demanding that the vegetarian supply the proof that a being has rights (assuming that sentiency might be such a condition),...perhaps the burden of proof should be on the meat-eater to justify his position in the light of the pain he causes.

Dombrowski, Daniel A. (Professor of Philosophy, Seattle University), *Vegetarianism: The Philosophy Behind the Ethical Diet*, 1985

It is my view that the vegetarian manner of living by its purely physical effect on the human temperament would most beneficially influence the lot of mankind.

Einstein, Dr. Albert, 1879-1955 (Nobel Prize-winning physicist), letter to *Vegetarian Watch-Tower*, December 1930

You have just dined, and however scrupulously the slaughterhouse is concealed in the graceful distance of miles, there is complicity.

Emerson, Ralph Waldo, 1803-1882 (American author and philosopher), *Fate*

There is no limit to the testimony of history on the physical, moral and religious advantages of non-flesh diet. Whether we listen to Greece or to Rome, to Egypt or Israel, to the Historian, the Philosopher, or to the Theologian, the message is the same....They have all discovered in every land that Higher Law of God written in the human heart and in nature, disobedience to which brings physical pain and corruption, moral dullness and inertia, spiritual blindness and impotence—the very things which now lie upon society like a nightmare.

Ferrier, J. Todd, 1855-1943, *On Behalf of the Creatures*

The key word to put back into our complex relationship with food is respect—for the lives of animals, for how foods are grown and harvested, for the conditions of those who do the harvesting and the preparing, and finally, for ourselves and our families and what we put into our bodies.

Fox, Nichols (Journalist), *Spoiled: The Dangerous Truth About a Food Chain Gone Haywire*, 1997

Something has changed in the degree to which fresh poultry, eggs, and meat are contaminated today, and those changes are at least partly the result of an arrogant and duplicitous meat and poultry industry that is banking its future on keeping consumers ignorant and complacent....What seems clear is that the cure must be as systemic as the cause, and it must involve a new consumer consciousness, a new caring about food that goes beyond the superficialities of transitory taste sensations to the very nature of food and how it is produced.

Ibid

The demand for butcher's meat may not seem materially lessened because I do not eat it, but it is lessened notwithstanding, and I rejoice to know that in the past seven years my abstinence from flesh must have resulted in a little less slaughter, and I am glad to have reduced by even one drop the depth of that ocean of blood.

Freshel, M. R. L., 1864-1949, *Golden Rule Cook-Book*

I do feel that spiritual progress does demand at some stage that we should cease to kill our fellow creatures for the

souls like ourselves

satisfaction of our bodily wants.

Gandhi, Mohandas Karamchand, 1869-1948, The Mahatma (Great Soul), *The Moral Basis of Vegetarianism*

If anybody said that I should die if I did not take beef-tea or mutton, even under medical advice, I would prefer death.

Gandhi, Mohandas Karamchand, 1869-1948, The Mahatma (Great Soul), address, November 20, 1931

I hold flesh-food to be unsuited to our species.

Gandhi, Mohandas Karamchand, 1869-1948, The Mahatma (Great Soul), *Mahatma Gandhi, His Mission and Message*

Until recently, many eyebrows would have been raised by suggesting that an imbalance of normal dietary components could lead to cancer and cardiovascular disease....Today, the accumulation of...evidence...makes this notion not only possible but certain....[The] dietary factors responsible [are] principally meat and fat intake.

Gori, Dr. Gio B. (Deputy Director of the National Cancer Institute's Division of Cancer Cause and Prevention), U.S. Senate Select Committee testimony, quoted in *The Vegetarian Alternative*, 1978

Everything we have learned about animals suggests that in terms of experiencing terror, pain, grief, anxiety and stress these sentient beings are relevantly similar to humans. It is reasonable to believe that our knowledge of the quality of human dying will also tell us something about the dying process of other animals. For humans, the most horrible deaths involve terror. When this factor is not present, and especially when the process of dying not unexpected for the dying person, dying can be peaceful. From this minimal observation about human dying and the observation that domestic animals are typically slaughtered in circumstances that are unfamiliar and terrifying for the animals, it follows that the experience of being slaughtered is no worse for these animals than the worst deaths experienced in the wild and significantly worse than the deaths of wild animals that die from disease or old age in familiar and unterrifying sur-roundings.

Gruzalski, Bart, Department of Philosophy and Religion,

Northeastern University, 'The Case Against Raising and Killing Animals For Food' in *Ethics and Animals*, eds. Miller and Williams, 1983

With respect to animal diet, let it be considered that taking away the lives of animals, in order to convert them into food, does great violence to the principles of benevolence and compassion.

Hartley, David, 1705-1757 (English physician and philosopher), *Observations on Man*

I'm a mother. I know. I have a pretty good idea of the kind of emotions that it would put me through to have somebody take my baby away from me. Now why, as even a remotely sensitive creature, would I wish to inflict that kind of suffering on any other creature—be it human or whatever? It's completely inhumane. There's no way you can justify it. There's no way anyone who has humanity or any compassion can stand here and take a calf away from its mother and think that that's all right.

Hynde, Chrissie (Musician), interview in *Vegetarian Times*, September 1987

Pythagoras enjoined abstinence from the flesh of animals because this was conducive to Peace. Those who are accustomed to abominate the slaughter of other animals, as iniquitous and unnatural, will think it still more unlawful and unjust to kill a man or engage in war.

Iamblichus, c. 250-325 (Syrian philosopher), *De Vita Pythagorica*

Our meat-centered diet and the large-scale animal agriculture that supports it, is devastating all the life support systems upon which we depend—the topsoil, the forests, the rivers, the ground water, the air and the oceans. Evolving our diet away from the current animal-based diet is arguably the single most effective action we can take as individuals and as a society to improve our health and to stabilize our endangered eco-system.

Klapper, Michael, M.D. (Physician and educator)

The following pages were written in the Concentration Camp

in Dachau, in the midst of all kinds of cruelties. They were furtively scrawled in a hospital barrack where I stayed during my illness, in a time when Death grasped day by day after us, when we lost twelve thousand within four and a half months....

'You asked me why I do not eat meat and you are wondering at the reasons of my behavior...I refuse to eat animals because I cannot nourish myself by the sufferings and by the death of other creatures. I refuse to do so, because I suffered so painfully myself that I can feel the pains of others by recalling my own sufferings....

'I am not preaching...I am writing this letter to you, to an already awakened individual who rationally controls his impulses, who feels responsible, internally and externally, for his acts, who knows that our supreme court is sitting in our conscience....

'I have not the intention to point out with my finger...I think it is much more my duty to stir up my own conscience....

'That is the point: I want to grow up into a better world where a higher law grants more happiness, in a new world where God's commandment reigns: You shall love each other.'

Kupfer, Edgar, "Animals, My Brethren," *The Dachau Diaries of Edgar Kupfer*, Special Collection of the Library of the University of Chicago

As soon as I realized that I didn't need meat to survive or to be in good health, I began to see how forlorn it all is. If only we had a different mentality about the drama of the cowboy and the range and all the rest of it. It's a very romantic notion, an entrenched part of American culture, but I've seen, for example, pigs waiting to be slaughtered, and their hysteria and panic was something I shall never forget for the rest of my life.

Leachman, Cloris (Actress), *The Vegetarians*

I venture to maintain that there are multitudes to whom the necessity of discharging the duties of a butcher would be so inexpressibly painful and revolting, that if they could obtain a flesh diet on no other condition, they would relinquish it for ever.

Lecky, W. E. H. (Irish historian), 1838-1903, *History of European Morals*

People should visit abattoirs and see for themselves whether what goes on in them is compatible with the spirit of Jesus.

Linzey, Reverend Dr. Andrew, Center for the Study of Theology, University of Essex, U.K., interview after visiting a Massachusetts slaughterhouse, 1988

We stopped eating meat the day we happened to look out our window during Sunday lunch and saw our young lambs playing happily, as kittens do, in the fields. Eating bits of them suddenly made no sense. In fact, it was revolting.

McCartney, Linda, 1942-1998 (Photographer and author), preface, *Save the Animals*, 1990

We don't eat anything that has to be killed for us. We've been through a lot and we've reached a stage where we really value life.

McCartney, Paul (Musician), interview, August 1984

The Utopians feel that slaughtering our fellow creatures gradually destroys the sense of compassion, which is the finest sentiment of which our human nature is capable.

More, Thomas, 1478-1535 (English humanist), *Utopia*, 1518

But for the sake of some little mouthful of flesh we deprive a soul of the sun and light, and of that proportion of life and time it had been born into the world to enjoy.

Plutarch, c. 46-120 (Greek biographer and author), *Moralia*

But to deliver animals to be slaughtered and cooked, and thus be filled with murder, not for the sake of nutriment and satisfying the wants of nature, but making pleasure and gluttony the end of such conduct, is transcendently iniquitous and dire.

Porphyry, 233-304 (Greek philosopher), *On Abstinence from Animal Food*

4. ANIMAL CONSUMPTION AND VEGETARIANISM

Alas, what wickedness to swallow flesh into our own flesh, to fatten our greedy bodies by cramming in other bodies, to have one living creature fed by the death of another! In the midst of such wealth as earth, the best of mothers, provides, nothing forsooth satisfies you, but to behave like the Cyclopes, inflicting sorry wounds with cruel teeth! You cannot appease the hungry cravings of your wicked, gluttonous stomachs except by destroying some other life.

Pythagoras, 6th century B.C. (Greek philosopher and mathematician), depicted in Ovid: *The Metamorphoses*

In the final analysis, there are compelling moral and spiritual reasons, apart from scriptural ones, to abstain from meat....Refraining from eating meat helps prevent cruelty to animals and promotes protection of the environment and the health of one's body, 'the temple of the Lord.' For all these reasons, a vegetarian diet is one good way of maintaining a life-style consistent with the humane and ecological spirit of the Scriptures.

Regenstein, Lewis G. (Director of the Interfaith Council for the Protection of Animals and Nature), *Replenish the Earth*, 1991

It takes less water to produce a year's food for a pure vegetarian than to produce a month's food for a meat-eater....The amount of water consumed by America's meat habit is staggering.

Robbins, John (Author), *Diet for a New America*, 1987

Throughout history there have been people who have chosen to be vegetarians because they did not feel it was right to kill animals for food when this was not necessary, when there was other nourishing food available. But today, because of the way animals are raised for market, the question of whether or not to eat meat has a whole new meaning, and a whole new urgency. Never before have animals been treated like this. Never before has such deep, unrelenting, and systematic cruelty been mass produced. Never before has the decision of each individual been so important.

Ibid

The world of science echoes the world's religions with its own equivalent of the Golden Rule. Newton's Third Law of Motion says that 'For every action, there is an equal and opposite reaction.' While Newton's law applies only to material nature, the implications run deeper still, extending to the most subtle levels of existence. In the East, this is called the law of karma....In a very fundamental sense, too, this law relates to our treatment of animals. The violence in society is at least in part the result of our merciless diet and abuse of the natural world around us. In karmic terms, violence begets violence. In dietary terms, you are what you eat.

Rosen, Steven (Author), *Food for the Spirit*, 1987

The basis of vegetarianism is ethical. It is a practical acknowledgment that the unnecessary killing of other creatures is barbarous. It has economic and health benefits. Being an obvious truth, the humanitarian idea is easy to grasp. No sensible person would claim that animal butchery is spiritually elevating or is anything but the opposite of all we hold beautiful and good.

Rudd, Geoffrey L., *The British Vegetarian*, January/February 1964

[On being asked why he was a vegetarian] Oh, come! That boot is on the other leg. Why should you call me to account for eating decently? If I battened on the scorched corpses of animals, you might well ask me why I did that.

Shaw, George Bernard, 1856-1950 (Nobel Prize-winning author), interview, January 15, 1898

I address myself not to the young enthusiast only, but to the ardent devotee of truth and virtue—the pure and passionate moralist yet unvitiated by the contagion of the world. He will embrace a pure system from its abstract truth, its beauty, its simplicity, and its promise of wide extended benefit. Unless custom has turned poison into food, he will hate the brutal pleasure of the chase by instinct. It will be a contemplation full of horror and disappointment to the mind that beings, capable of the gentlest and most admirable sympathies, would take delight in the death pangs and last convulsions of dying animals.

Shelley, Percy Bysshe, 1792-1822 (English poet), *A Vindication of Natural Diet*

The longer I am a vegetarian, the more I feel how wrong it is to kill animals and eat them. I think that eating meat or fish is a denial of all ideals, even of all religions.

Singer, Isaac Bashevis, 1904-1991 (Nobel Prize-winning author), quoted in *Replenish the Earth*, 1991

When a human kills an animal for food, he is neglecting his own hunger for justice. Man prays for mercy, but is unwilling to extend it to others. Why should man then expect mercy from God? It's unfair to expect something that you are not willing to give.

Singer, Isaac Bashevis, 1904-1991 (Nobel Prize-winning author), preface to *Food for the Spirit*, 1987

For most humans, especially those in modern urban and suburban communities, the most direct form of contact with non-human animals is at meal time: we eat them. This simple fact is the key to our attitudes to other animals, and also the key to what each one of us can do about changing these attitudes. The use and abuse of animals raised for food far exceeds, in sheer numbers of animals affected, any other kind of mistreatment. Hundreds of millions of cattle, pigs, and sheep are raised and slaughtered in the United States alone each year; and for poultry the figure is a staggering three billion. (That means that about 5000 birds—mostly chickens—will have been slaughtered in the time it takes you to read this page.) It is here, on our dinner table and in our neighborhood supermarket or butcher's shop, that we are brought into direct touch with the most extensive exploitation of other species that has ever existed.

Singer, Peter, Ph.D. (Professor of Philosophy, Monash University, Australia), *Animal Liberation*, 1975

Those who, by their purchases, require animals to be killed have no right to be shielded from the slaughterhouse or any other aspect of the production of the meat they buy. If it is distasteful for humans to think about, what can it be like for the animals to experience it?

Ibid

We consume the carcasses of creatures of like appetites, passions and organs with our own, and fill the slaughterhouses daily with screams of pain and fear.

Stevenson, Robert Louis, 1850-1894 (Scottish author)

I believe that every man who has ever been earnest to preserve his higher or poetic faculties in the best condition has been particularly inclined to abstain from animal food, and from much food of any kind.

Thoreau, Henry D., 1817-1862 (American poet and philosopher), *Walden*

I have no doubt that it is a part of the destiny of the human race, in its gradual improvement, to leave off eating animals, as surely as the savage tribes have left off eating each other when they came in contact with the more civilized.

Ibid

Auntie was fond of food and when she was offered only a vegetarian diet she was indignant, said she could not eat any old filth and demanded that they give her meat, chicken. The next time she came to dinner she was astonished to find a live chicken tied to her chair and a large knife at her plate.

Tolstoy, Alexandra, *Tolstoy: A Life of My Father*

The Vegetarian movement ought to fill with gladness the souls of those who have at heart the realization of God's kingdom upon earth, not because Vegetarianism itself is such an important step towards the realization of this kingdom (all real steps are equally important or unimportant), but because it serves as a criterion by which we know that the pursuit of moral perfection on the part of man is genuine and sincere.

Tolstoy, Leo Nikolayevich, 1828-1910 (Russian novelist), *News Review*, 1892

A man can live and be healthy without killing animals for food; therefore, if he eats meat, he participates in taking animal life merely for the sake of his appetite. And to act so is immoral.

Tolstoy, Leo Nikolayevich, 1828-1910 (Russian novelist), *On Civil Disobedience*

Not long ago I also had a talk with a retired soldier, a butcher, and he too was surprised by my assertion that it was a pity to kill, and said the usual things about its being ordained; but afterwards he agreed with me: 'Especially when they are quiet, tame cattle. They come, poor things, trusting you. It is very pitiful.'...This is dreadful! Not the suffering and death of the animals, but that man suppresses in himself, unnecessarily, the highest spiritual capacity—that of sympathy and pity toward living creatures like himself—and by violating his own feelings becomes cruel. And how deeply seated in the human heart is the injunction not to take life! But by the assertion that God ordained the slaughter of animals, and above all as a result of habit, people entirely lose their natural feeling.

Tolstoy, Leo Nikolayevich, 1828-1910 (Russian novelist), *The First Step*

I have from an early age abjured the use of meat, and the time will come when men such as I will look upon the murder of animals as they now look upon the murder of men.

Vinci, Leonardo da, 1452-1519 (Italian Renaissance artist), from da Vinci's *Notes*

Truly man is the king of beasts, for his brutality exceeds theirs. We live by the death of others: We are burial places!

Vinci, Leonardo da, 1452-1519 (Italian Renaissance artist), Merijkowsky, *Romance of Leonardo da Vinci*

Everyone in the world could have adequate food if the enormously wasteful habit of eating meat and its by-products was sacrificed by the richer minority of the earth's inhabitants who insist upon this totally unnecessary and unnatural diet....The only eco-logical next step for truly concerned observers of the world's predicament is to cease to consume meat and other animal products.

Wynne-Tyson, Jon (English author and publisher), *The Civilised Alternative*, 1972

souls like ourselves

5. FARM ANIMALS AND FACTORY FARMING

*N*o other farm animal endures such extreme and prolonged physical confinement and crowding as the laying hen.

Adcock, Melanie, D.V.M. (Veterinarian), interview, 1993

Newborn dairy calves are typically taken from their mothers at birth or shortly thereafter. Some female calves are kept as replacements for individuals in the dairy herd. The other calves are sent to slaughter as babies, to veal farms, or to be raised for beef. Many are sent to stockyards when only one or two days old, even before they can walk.

Adcock, Melanie, D.V.M. (Veterinarian), 1995

The fifth foal I bid on had crooked legs, was skinny and she wobbled onto the auction scale by herself. She was deformed. She held her head high and looked at the bidders. Her facial expression came across as one who was resigned to her fate. My heart went out to her. I bought her. One of the buyers beside me was disgusted with me and told me so. It took all of my energies to maintain my composure and hold back the tears. During the bidding, some men were sent over to try to intimidate me....The banging of the heavy steel doors when the foals came onto the scale, the noise as the foals were yelled at and prodded, made me cringe. Sheer terror came over their faces. Their tiny bodies shook with fright. Some of the foals lost control of their bodily functions while on the scale, only to get sworn at....As I am writing this down, I feel a white hot rage burn inside of me as to the cruelty involved in this PMU [pregnant mare's urine] industry....

Anonymous foal rescuer, 1998

Whenever people say 'We mustn't be sentimental,' you can take it they are about to do something cruel. And if they add 'We must be realistic,' they mean they are going to make money out of it. These slogans have a long history. After being used to justify slave traders, ruthless industrialists, and contractors who had found that the most economically 'realistic' method of cleaning a chimney was to force a small child to climb it, they have now been passed on, like an heirloom, to the factory farmers....'We mustn't be sentimental' tries to persuade us that factory farming isn't, in fact, cruel. It implies that the whole problem has been invented by our sloppy imaginations. The factory farmers dare not quite claim that animals are incapable of feeling. The public can't be relied on to be quite so ignorant. After all, anyone who is personally acquainted with a dog, cat or canary has as much evidence that mammals and birds can feel pain, terror or misery as he has in the case of his fellow citizens....'We must be realistic,' on the other hand, tacitly admits that factory farming is cruel but seeks to make us believe it is economically necessary. Sometimes we are even told we mustn't resist it because it is an 'advanced' method—a theory on which we ought to have welcomed Auschwitz as a great step forward in gas technology. It used to be said, of course, that slavery was economically necessary. Since we've dared to put it to the test, we've discovered that it isn't, and that we are quite ingenious enough to manage without it. But of course, even if slavery were a hundred times more economically advantageous than freedom, we couldn't, as moral and imaginative beings, tolerate it. *No more can we tolerate factory farming. It is as indefensible as the slave trade, and it is our business to make it as unthinkable.*

Brophy, Brigid, 1929-1995 (British novelist), *Unlived Life—A Manifesto Against Factory Farming*

Gone are the pastoral scenes in which animals wandered through green fields or flocks of chickens scratched contentedly for their food. In their place are factorylike buildings in which animals live out their wretched existences without ever feeling the earth beneath their feet, without knowing sunlight, or experiencing the simple pleasures of grazing for natural food—indeed, so confined or so intolerably crowded that movement of any kind is scarcely possible.

Carson, Rachel, 1907-1964 (Biologist and author), quoted in
Factory Farming: The Experiment That Failed, 1987

The fact is, animals are given more care and consideration when they are dead—as carcass meat—than when they are alive.

Coats, C. David, *Old MacDonald's Factory Farm*, 1989

From the beginnings of domestication of animals, interest in their freedom from suffering has been subordinated to economic considerations....But with the advent of factory farming, the evil has been terribly accentuated.

Cobb, John B. (Theologian and author), quoted in *Eating with Conscience*, 1997

I am a battery hen. I live in a cage so small I cannot stretch my wings. I am forced to stand night and day on a sloping wire mesh floor that painfully cuts into my feet. The cage walls tear my feathers, forming blood blisters that never heal. The air is so full of ammonia that my lungs hurt and my eyes burn and I think I am going blind. As soon as I was born, a man grabbed me and sheared off part of my beak with a hot iron, and my little brothers were thrown into trash bags as useless alive....Humans, I wish I were dead, and soon I will be dead. Look for pieces of my wounded flesh wherever chicken pies and soups are sold.

Davis, Karen, Ph.D. (President, United Poultry Concerns),
"Thinking Like a Chicken," *In Animals & Women*, 1995

The poet William Blake said that we must learn to see the universe in a grain of sand. We must learn with equal justice and perception to hear the music of the spheres in the cluck of a chicken....

Ibid

As a veterinary student in England some forty years ago, I worked on traditional farms. The animals included free-range sheep, dairy cows, poultry, pigs, and beef cattle....The animals were free to be themselves, and most of the farmers had great affection for both their animals and the land....In

1978 I walked into a 'factory farm' for the first time. It was a small battery-hen egg factory. Soon after that I visited a small hog-confinement building. I was in a state of suspended disbelief, bordering on shock. In the nearly twenty years since then, I have visited much larger factories, dairy and beef cattle feedlots, as well as auction yards and slaughterhouses. I am still horrified by the inhumane treatment of animals and still shocked by the unhealthy conditions for humans and the environment.

Fox, Michael W., D.Sc., Ph.D., B.Vet.Med. (Ethologist), *Eating with Conscience*, 1997

We cannot bring ourselves to regard close confinement of sows by stalls or tethers throughout their pregnancies—which is, for most of their adult lives—with anything but distaste....

Great Britain's House of Commons' Agricultural Committee, report, 1981

In fact if one person is unkind to an animal it is considered to be cruelty, but where a lot of people are unkind to animals, especially in the name of commerce, the cruelty is condoned and, once large sums of money are at stake, will be defended to the last by otherwise intelligent people.

Harrison, Ruth (British author), *Animal Machines*, 1964

Veal calf producers talk readily enough of cruelty, even admit that some of their methods are inhumane, but offer you [the] flimsy excuse that they are only producing *what the public wants*. We must cease to pander to an unenlightened public. We have laws to punish perverted and ignorant children who torture animals because it gives them pleasure; it is time we applied these laws to causing suffering to animals because their carcasses then are said to tickle our palates.

Ibid

A ride to Brighton yesterday morning, it being the day of the weekly cattle fair. William Allen and myself went in a wagon, carrying a calf to be sold at the fair. The calf had not had his breakfast, as his mother had preceded him to Brighton; and he kept expressing his hunger and discomfort by loud, sonorous baas, especially when we passed any cattle in the fields or on the road. The cows grazing within hearing expressed great interest, and some of them came galloping to the roadside to behold the calf....He was a prettily behaved urchin and kept thrusting his hairy muzzle between William and myself, apparently wishing to be stroked and petted. It was an ugly thought, that his confidence in human nature, and Nature in general, was to be so ill rewarded as by cutting his throat and selling him in quarters.

Hawthorne, Nathaniel, 1804-1864 (American novelist), *The American Notebooks*

[Regarding the production of Premarin from pregnant mare's urine (PMU)] The doomsday clock is again well on its way for tens of thousands of innocent [horses'] lives—lives that, once again, will end in terror needlessly. With a few strokes of the prescribing pen, we are able to decide the fate of future innocents....It comes down to a simple choice. It is also a choice that speaks worlds—about us.

Kellosalmi, R. M., M.D., "Inhumanity By Prescription," *Family Practice*, May 8, 1995

Confining a de-beaked hen in a battery cage is more than a moral crime; it is a living sign of our failure to recognize the blessing of God in creation.

Linzey, Reverend Dr. Andrew, Center for the Study of Theology, University of Essex, U.K., *Christianity and the Rights of Animals*, 1987

A visit to a milk-fed veal factory in northern Connecticut gave us a feel for the business of veal production. Although it was broad daylight outside, the calves' rooms were pitch-dark; our guide explained that darkness helped keep the calves quieter. At feeding time the lights were turned on as the producer made his rounds. In two rooms, more than a hundred calves were crated in rows of wooden stalls. Their eyes followed our movements; some appeared jittery, others lethargic. Many tried to stretch toward us from their stalls in an attempt to suckle a finger, a hand, or part of our clothing. The farmer explained: 'They want their mothers, I guess.'

Mason, Jim (Journalist and author) and **Peter Singer, Ph.D.**
(Professor of Philosophy, Monash University, Australia), *Animal
Factories*, 1980

Six blank-eyed pigs, lying comatose on a thin mat of dirty
straw, appear to be near death in a windswept pen at the
South St. Paul [Minnesota] Livestock Market. The animals,
closer to being deadstock than livestock, are scheduled to be
hauled away to a slaughterhouse in a few days. Their
butchered, sliced and cellophaned corpses will be sold as
bacon, ham and sausage, the eaters all but oblivious to the
horror and sorrow of the animals' last days....This market—a
sprawling mall of loading docks, chutes, pens and crates—is
America's second-largest animal auction. It is a transfer sta-
tion between farms and slaughterhouses and where some 1
million cattle, calves and pigs are penned, handled and sold
annually....Some [animals] break a leg when being electrically
prodded onto trucks, others are felled by exhaustion from the
extreme cold or heat of the farm-to-market haul. Once
downed, the animals are usually abandoned in 'cripple
chutes,' later to be roped and dragged to a slaughterhouse-
bound truck....Tears need to be shed. Habits, too.

McCarthy, Colman (Columnist, *The Washington Post*), 1991

Anyone who has studied the social life of birds carefully will
know that theirs is a subtle and complex world, where food
and water are only a small part of their behavioral needs. The
brain of each bird is programmed with a complicated set of
drives and responses which set it on the path to a life full of
special territorial, nesting, roosting, grooming, parental,
aggressive and sexual activities, in addition to the feeding
behavior. All of these activities are totally denied the battery
hens.

Morris, Dr. Desmond (English animal behaviorist), 1983

PMU [pregnant mare's urine] horses and foals can be spared
lives of misery if women choose plant-derived or synthetic
estrogen products instead of Premarin....Women do not have
to choose between their health and their consciences when
faced with the issue of hormone replacement....Every woman

has a choice and every choice will make a difference.

Paulhus, Mark (Director, Equine Protection, The Humane
Society of the United States), 1996

All of today's food animals—the proud and passionate
chickens, the friendly and steadfast pigs, the gentle-hearted
cows—are treated today in a manner that would, I believe,
sicken any open-hearted person who had eyes to see what
was actually happening....I don't know what shall be the des-
tinies of those responsible for the animal factories of today.
But regardless of the future, it is already sadly true that they
live in a heartless world. Treating animals like machines, they
are profoundly separated from nature, deeply alienated from
kinship with life. They are already in a kind of hell....If we
buy and eat the products of this system of food production
are we not colluding with them in creating this hell?

Robbins, John (Author) *Diet for a New America*, 1987

Today's chicken farms are not really 'farms' any more, but
should more accurately be called 'chicken factories.'
Factories, because the chickens live their whole lives inside
buildings entirely devoid of natural light....Factories,
because these proud and sensitive creatures are treated
strictly as merchandise, with utter contempt for their spirits,
with not a trace of feeling or compassion for the fact that
they are living, breathing animals. Factories, because the
chickens are systematically deprived of every conceivable
expression of their natural urges....We are a nation with an
assembly-line chicken in every pot. We do not know that we
eat the bodies and eggs of tortured creatures.

Ibid

Deprived not only of their mothers, but of any conceivable
source of stimulation and interest, the little baby calves crave
something to suck on....If you move close to a veal calf's head,
he will try frantically to suck on your hand, or your elbow, or
your shirt, or your purse, or your umbrella, or anything at all
he can reach. It is hard to avoid feeling that these calves in
bondage are not veal machines, but ill little babies, desperately
craving for what might heal their disease.

Ibid

souls like ourselves

The powerful agribusiness and pharmaceutical lobbies have seen to it that farm animals are explicitly excluded from the federal Animal Welfare Act. There are virtually no laws which protect farm animals from even the most harsh and brutal treatment as long as it takes place in the name of production and profit. It is left entirely to the preference of the individual company how many egg-laying hens are stuffed into each little wire cage, or whether an artificially inseminated sow must spend her entire pregnancy chained to the floor of a cement-bottomed cage.

The Humane Farming Association, *Consumer Alert: The Dangers of Factory Farming*, 1985

souls like ourselves

6. ANIMAL RESEARCH AND TESTING

$\mathcal{T}$he standard carcinogen tests that use rodents are an obsolescent relic of the ignorance of past decades.

Abelson, Philip H., "Testing for Carcinogens With Rodents," *Science*, September 21, 1990

...I had bought two male chimps from a primate colony in Holland. They lived next to each other in separate cages for the several months before I used one as a donor. When we put him to sleep in his cage in preparation for the operation, he chattered and cried incessantly. We attached no significance to this, but it must have made a great impression on his companion, for when we removed the body to the operating room, the other chimp wept bitterly and was inconsolable for days. The incident made a deep impression on me. I vowed never again to experiment with such sensitive creatures.

Barnard, Dr. Christiaan (Cardiac surgeon), *Good Life Good Death*, 1980

In retrospect, I realize that the slow changes in my perception of the research I was doing were accompanied by changes on the empathic, as well as on the intellectual level. For example, on several occasions during the sixteen years I did research on non-human primates, I took it upon myself to destroy irradiated animals. Although not trained as a physiologist, I found I had the facility to locate a vein while many technicians could not. Rather than cause the monkey further suffering, I began to fill in when the veterinarian was absent. On each occasion a thought occurred to me: 'Do I have the "right" to do this?' I know now that a subliminal voice answered 'No!' but I felt I had no choice....I only hope that in changing my own views

75

I have become able to bring about similar changes in the views of those who unthinkingly continue to experiment today.

Barnes, Donald J., Ph.D. (Psychologist), "A Matter of Change," *In Defense of Animals*, 1985

The question of vivisection, which may be defined as the subjection of animals to experiments in the pursuit of scientific knowledge or commercial manufacture, is primarily a moral one, and it is upon this ground that I oppose it; for I refuse to believe that the pathway of true progress in human knowledge for the attainment of health can demand for its treading the infliction of pain and suffering upon beings weaker than ourselves, but sharing with us that One Life which animates all creatures.

Bayly, Dr. M. Beddow, MRCS, LRCP, 1887-1961, *Spotlights on Vivisection*

In a universe which embraces all types of life and consciousness and all material forms through which these manifest, nothing which is ethically wrong can ever be scientifically right; in an integrated cosmos of spirit and matter, one law must pervade all levels and all planes. This is the basic principle upon which the whole case against vivisection rests.

Bayly, Dr. M. Beddow, MRCS, LRCP, 1887-1961, *The Futility of Experiments on Animals*

I believe it is imperative to remind ourselves that progress in the understanding and management of human disease must begin and end with studies in man. Hepatitis serves as an example of how observations on human beings have clarified the different clinical expressions, the nature of the causative agents, the modes of their dissemination, and some measures of prevention of the disease....Hepatitis, although an almost pure example of progress by study in man, is by no means unusual, in fact, it is more nearly the rule.

Beeson, Paul B., M.D., Department of Medicine, University of Washington, "The growth of knowledge about a disease: Hepatitis." *American Journal of Medicine*, 1979; 67:366-370

The physiologist is not an ordinary man: he is a scientist, possessed and absorbed by the scientific idea that he pursues.

He does not hear the cries of animals, he does not see their flowing blood, he sees nothing but an organism that conceals from him the problem he is seeking to solve.

Bernard, Claude, 1813-1878 (French physiologist), *Introduction to the Study of Experimental Medicine*

If hospital service makes young students less tender to suffering, vivisection deadens their humanity and begets indifference to it.

Bigelow, Henry J., M.D., 1818-1890 (Former Professor of Physiology, Harvard University) *An Ethical Problem*

There will come a time when the world will look back to modern vivisection in the name of Science, as they do now to burning at the stake in the name of religion.

Bigelow, Henry J., M.D., 1818-1890 (Former Professor of Physiology, Harvard University), *Surgical Anaesthesia*

Why do we object to experiments of a certain kind whether on human beings or on animals? We object to them because they debase the man who does them so that he does not remain capable of making an objective judgment. Some of the people from whom I got a sense of science were men of enormous humanity—they were men in whom the knowledge of nature was a sense of love, a sense of devotion, a sense of dedication.

Bronowski, Dr. Jacob, 1908-1974 (British mathematician), *Science and Human Values*, 1956

A medical profession founded on callousness to the pain of the other animals may eventually destroy its own sensibility to the pain of humans.

Brophy, Brigid, 1929-1995 (British novelist), *Animals, Men and Morals*

The fact that there are bigger injustices and wrongs doesn't make it right to sacrifice an innocent monkey. It doesn't alter the case at all.

Brophy, Brigid, 1929-1995 (British novelist), *Hackenfeller's Ape*

I despise and abhor the pleas on behalf of that infamous

practice, vivisection....I would rather submit to the worst of deaths, so far as pain goes, than have a single dog or cat tortured on the pretense of sparing me a twinge or two.

Browning, Robert, 1812-1899 (English poet), from a letter

What we are saying if we support experimentation on animals is this: 'I would like to eat, wash in, inhale, drink, wear, or in some other way use a certain substance (which the human race has survived without, or with, for millions of years), but I am frightened what nasty effect the substance may have on me. Therefore, I will try it out on something weaker than myself who cannot refuse or object, so that if that someone screams, becomes ill, or dies, then I know not to use that substance.' That is cowardice!

Bryant, John M. (English engineer), *Fettered Kingdoms*, 1982

But of one thing I am convinced; that to take a dog—the most loving and trusting of creatures—and submit it, for whatever high-sounding end, to torture, physical and mental, must be vile and base. To the argument that such torture to a sentient and defenseless creature helps to preserve human life and alleviate human pain, I can only reply by saying that if my life could only be preserved on the condition of having such torture inflicted on a dog, I hope I should be man enough to refuse to keep it on such terms. And if I did not, I know I should feel utterly ashamed of myself. If we were put into the world to exist on such a basis, all our talk about humanitarianism has no real meaning.

Bryant, Sir Arthur (Wynne Morgan), 1899-1985 (British historian)

Those who are morally sensitive enough to feel revolted at the notion of vivisection, are often confused when faced with the indisputable argument that human lives can be saved as the results of these experiments. 'Which are more valuable,' it is asked, 'dogs or humans?' To which the answer, of course, is 'Dogs, if the humans are so inhuman as to torture dogs in order to save their own miserable skins.'

Byrom, Michael (English author), *Evolution for Beginners*

The opinion that man can gain real advance by betraying

and sacrificing an innocent fellow creature is exactly this. He may truly gain a mere point of technical information, but with regard to the true, the divine knowledge that he and the creature he torments are one, and that he cannot inflict injury on it without bringing injury and suffering on himself—with regard to this knowledge, which is to the other as the sun in heaven is to a farthing candle in a cellar, he is in gross and thick darkness. Every time he pins the trembling rabbit down to the operating table he draws a fresh veil between himself and the source of all Life and Light, and in the name of Knowledge confirms himself in pitiful blindness and ignorance.

Carpenter, Edward,1844-1929 (English social reform writer), *Vivisection*

After years of strife, the careerists of science are clearly ahead, largely because they are adept in arousing fearful and self-regarding thoughts among the lay public by threatening a new Dark Age for medicine if there is any curtailment of their absolute freedom.

Carson, Gerald (American author), *Man, Beasts, and Gods*, 1972

You can have a business that's socially responsible as well as successful. It's really unnecessary to keep testing and retesting.

Chappel, Kate, Tom's of Maine, quoted in *Victims of Vanity*, 1989

Science is wonderfully equipped to answer the question 'How?' but it gets terribly confused when you ask the question 'Why?'

Chargaff, Erwin, Ph.D. (Biochemist and author), *Columbia Forum*, 1969

It is more profitable to continue cancer research and violate more lives—animals, plants, and humans—than to eliminate the major carcinogenic materials that pour out from the vast industrial complex considered *vital* to a *healthy* economy.

Collard, Andrée, *Rape of the Wild*, 1989

Science can only ascertain what *is*, but not what *should be*, and outside of its domain value judgments of all kinds remain necessary.

Einstein, Dr. Albert, 1879-1955 (Nobel Prize-winning physicist), *Out of My Later Years*, 1950

The general public has been swayed by proponents' claims that animal tests protect them from harmful substances when in fact their efficacy is impossible to establish due to lack of corresponding human data....Revolutions in chemical testing and screening technologies have produced methods that are faster, cheaper and often superior to animal tests in terms of their accuracy when compared with human toxicity data.

Fano, Alix (Writer), *Lethal Laws*, 1997

We should keep in mind that the pharmaceutic and cosmetic industries torture, maim and sacrifice thousands of animals daily for what are economic rather than scientific reasons....As a naive medical student, I witnessed the forced feeding, blood-letting, killing and dissection of hundreds of dogs in order that a major drug company could back up minor charges in its television advertisements for aspirin.

Fiscella, Robert, M.D., letter, November 9, 1981

It was Washoe [chimpanzee] who taught me that 'human' is only an adjective that describes 'being,' and that the essence of who I am is not my humanness but my beingness. There are human beings, chimpanzee beings, and cat beings. The distinctions I had once drawn between such beings—distinctions that permitted one species to imprison and experiment on another species—were no longer morally defensible for me.

Fouts, Roger, Ph.D. (Professor of Psychology, Central Washington University), *Next of Kin: What Chimpanzees Have Taught Me About Who We Are*, 1997

Compassion does not and should not stop at the imagined barriers between species. Something is wrong with a system that exempts people from anticruelty laws just because those people happen to be wearing white lab coats. Science that dissociates itself from the pain of others soon becomes monstrous. Good science must be conducted with the head and the heart. Biomedical doctors have strayed too far from the guiding principle of the Hippocratic oath, 'First, do no harm.' Hippocrates was not referring only to humans. 'The soul is the same in all living creatures,' he said, 'although the body of each is different.'

Ibid

In the present state of the art, making quantitative assessments of human risk from animal experiments has little scientific merit.

Freedman, D. A., and **H. Zeisel** (Statisticians), "From Mouse-to-Man: The Quantitative Assessment of Cancer Risks," *Statistical Science* 3 (1988): 3-56

Vivisection is the blackest of all the black crimes that man is at present committing against God and His fair creation. It ill becomes us to invoke in our daily prayers the blessings of God, the Compassionate, if we in turn will not practise elementary compassion towards our fellow creatures.

Gandhi, Mohandas Karamchand, 1869-1948, The Mahatma (Great Soul), *The Moral Basis of Vegetarianism*

I believe the most valuable things we have learned through animal experimentation are insights into the human mentality. These insights have arisen from direct analysis of researchers at work, not from tenuous extrapolations to ourselves based on animal behavior in highly artificial laboratory environments. We have learned that otherwise compassionate people can become remarkably desensitized and detached from the suffering they inflict upon animals. We have learned that highly intelligent people can be engaged in the most trivial or eccentric research yet convince themselves that their work is important.

Ginnelli, Michael A., Ph.D. (Psychologist), in *Advances in Animal Welfare Science*, 1985/86

As biomedical researchers we have tended to identify ourselves and our work with the finest exemplars of animal research. This is natural enough and can be seen as an attempt to self-motivate to a higher level of professional performance. But when it is made to appear that these examples are typical of the quality and usefulness of animal research, we have entered the domain of strict strategic action. Worst of all, this dogma may become something we ourselves begin to believe....The evidence is clear that all is not as well as we wish or as well as we represent to the public.

Gluck, J. P., and **S. R. Kubacki** (Research scientists), "Animals in biomedical research: the undermining effect of the rhetoric of the besieged," *Ethics and Behavior*, 1: 157-73, 1991

Once one accepts that there is something essentially different between a dog chasing after a stick and a stone plummeting to earth, then one will have a hard time in morally justifying, for example, why a healthy dog is given lung cancer with tobacco smoke in order to prove something to a suicidal human who smokes forty cigarettes a day.

Godlovitch, Stanley (Philosopher), *Animals, Men and Morals*, 1972

I watched, with shock, anger and anguish, a videotape...revealing the conditions in a large biomedical research laboratory, under contract to the National Institutes of Health, in which various primates, including chimpanzees, are maintained. I was given permission to visit the facility....It was a visit I shall never forget. Room after room was lined with small, bare cages, stacked one above the other, in which monkeys circled round and round and chimpanzees sat huddled, far gone in depression and despair. Young chimpanzees, 3 or 4 years old, were crammed, two together, into tiny cages measuring 22 inches by 22 inches and only 24 inches high. They could hardly turn around. Not yet part of any experiment, they have been confined in these cages for more than three months. The chimps had each other for comfort, but they would not remain together for long. Once they are infected, probably with hepatitis, they will be separated and placed in another cage. And there they will remain, living in conditions of severe sensory deprivation, for the next several years. During that time, they will become insane. A juvenile female rocked from side to side, sealed off from the outside world behind the glass doors of her metal isolation chamber. She was in semidarkness. All she could hear was the incessant roar of air rushing through vents into her prison....I shall be haunted forever by her eyes....

Goodall, Jane, Ph.D. (Ethologist), interview, May 17, 1987

Unfortunately, extrapolation from animal results to man remains largely problematical and no amount of mathematical sophistication can render such extrapolation more certain.

Higginson, J., and **C. S. Muir**, International Agency for Research on Cancer, "The Role of Epidemiology in Elucidating the Importance of Environmental Factors in Human Cancer," *Cancer Detection and Prevention* 1: 81, 1976

We may subject mice, or other laboratory animals, to such an atmosphere of tobacco smoke that they can—like the old man in the fairy story—neither sleep nor slumber; they can neither breed nor eat. And lung cancers may or may not develop to a significant degree. What then? We may have thus strengthened the evidence, we may even have narrowed the search, but we must, I believe, invariably return to man for the final proof or proofs.

Hill, A. Bradford, D.Sc., Ph.D. (Professor of Medical Statistics, London School of Hygiene), "Observation and experiment," *New England Journal of Medicine*, 248: 995-1001,1953

In conclusion, it appears that, for political reasons, the historical value of animal research has been grossly overstated. Not all animal research is irrelevant, but its value is severely limited by anatomical, physiological, and pathological differences between people and nonhuman animals. Most of the billions of dollars invested annually in animal research could be used much more effectively in clinical research or public health programs.

Kaufman, Stephen, M.D. (Ophthalmologist), "*Most Animal Research Is Not Beneficial to Human Health*," position paper, December 18, 1988

The issue of animal experimentation has a profound moral dimension to it. In this area, more than in any other, we speak and act for those who have no means of defending themselves. Not just their welfare, but their lives are in our hands....Public disillusionment with science in general is increasing year by year. Never before has there been such a tide of moral outrage over what we have seen and heard is happening in our Nation's laboratories. However, what we face today is not a crusade against science per se. Rather, it

souls like ourselves

is a movement set on defining our needs and determining how best to fill them without resorting to inhumane and uncivilized means. It is a sign that we are entering a new age of social and ethical considerations, for we now seek knowledge and benefit uncontaminated by brutality.

Lantos, Tom (United States Congressman), from a speech in the House of Representatives, March 22, 1983, *Congressional Record*, Vol. 129, No. 37

The one or two or three hundred millions of dollars a year that we're now spending on routine animal tests are almost worthless....it is simply not possible with all the animals in the world to go through new chemicals in the blind way that we have at the present time, and reach credible conclusions about the hazards to human health.

Lederberg, Joshua, M.D. (Nobel Prize-winning geneticist and microbiologist), *Chemical and Engineering News*, March 2: 5, 1981

Animal tests are no guarantee of safety in humans. I know of no physician who relies on these tests in deciding treatment for cases of accidental poisoning.

Lees, David, M.D., as quoted in *Victims of Vanity*, 1989

If we cut up beasts simply because they cannot prevent us and because we are backing our own side in the struggle for existence, it is only logical to cut up imbeciles, criminals, enemies, or capitalists for the same reasons.

Lewis, C. S. (British scholar, novelist and author), 1898-1963, *The Problem of Pain*, 1962

The clearer it became to me that animals have deep feelings, the more outraged I grew at the thought of any kind of animal experimentation. Can we justify these experiments when we know what animals feel as they undergo these tortures?

Masson, Jeffrey Moussaieff, Ph.D., prologue, *When Elephants Weep*, 1995

In most cases, the animal tests cannot predict what will happen when the drug is given to man. Standards for toxicology are often set by officials such as Federal regulators, who are responding to the pressures of ill-advised but obviously well-intended legislators or consumer groups who may or may not be aware of the futility of increasing the amount of testing required when some tests often have no bearing on how man will respond to the drug. The result is not only a waste of animals but also a waste of limited scientific resource; the loss is compounded by the fact that human life will not benefit from drugs whose release is unnecessarily delayed.

Melmon, K. L., *Clin Pharmacol Ther,* 20: 125-129, 1976

Extrapolation from the animal mode to humans represents something of a leap of faith.

Office of Science & Technology Policy, *Identification, Characterization, and Control of Potential Carcinogens: A Framework for Federal Decision-Making*, Washington, DC, February 1979

It is now realised that chemical toxicity and carcinogenicity are the consequence of the metabolic formation of 1) reactive intermediates and/or 2) reactive oxygen species (ROS) from the toxic chemical. Glutathione (GSH) protects against both, but rodents unlike man do not conserve their GSH, and use it in detoxification processes where man uses water. Moreover, rodents, having a high body surface area to body mass and therefore a much higher respiratory quotient than man, generate ROS much more extensively than occurs in man, and consequently experience GSH depletion, oxidative stress, malignancy and death at doses of chemicals that are non-toxic to humans. This has been known for at least a decade, but it is often ignored for the sake of tradition, convenience and economy.

Parke, Dennis V. (Emeritus Professor of Biochemistry, University of Surrey, U.K.) "Ethical Aspects of the Safety of Medicines and Other Social Chemicals," *Science & Engineering Ethics I*, 3: 291, 1995

Over and over researchers assured me that in their laboratories, animals were never hurt....Scientists could tell me these things with apparent conviction because they defined pain and suffering very narrowly. 'Pain' meant the acute pain of surgery on conscious animals, and almost nothing else. When I went beyond the issue of physical pain to ask about psychological or emotional suffering, many researchers were at a loss to answer....Researchers believe that all animals are capable of feeling pain, but what they actually see when they look at lab animals is a scientific objective, not the animal's subjective experience. The result is that it rarely occurs to them to consider whether an animal is in pain, is suffering — or whether it is feeling anything at all, outside the boundaries of the research protocol.

> **Philips, M.**, "Savages, drunks and lab animals," *Society and Animals*, 1: 61-81, 1993

Any work which seeks to elucidate the cause of a disease, the mechanism of a disease, the cure of disease, or the prevention of disease, must begin and end with observations on man, whatever the intermediate steps may be.

> **Pickering, Sir George, M.D.** (Professor of Medicine, University of London), "Opportunity and the universities," *Lancet*, 2: 895-898, 1952

The idea, as I understand it, is that fundamental truths are revealed in laboratory experimentation on lower animals and are then applied to the problem of the sick patient. Having been myself trained as a physiologist, I feel in a way competent to assess such a claim. It is plain nonsense.

> **Pickering, Sir George, M.D.** (Professor of Medicine, University of London) *British Medical Journal*, December 26, 1964

I think there's something more than pain in a lot of these experiments that I object to. I think there's misery. I think it's a wretched state to see an animal wasting away, perhaps with vomiting or diarrhea, miserable in its cage. No amount of testing can make a drug absolutely safe, if only because humans react differently from animals.

> **Platt, Lord Robert, M.Sc., M.D.**, 1900-1978, Presidential address, Royal College of Physicians

What is the importance of human lives? Is it their continuing alive for so many years like animals in a menagerie? The value of a man cannot be judged by the number of diseases from which he escapes. The value of a man is in his human qualities: in his character, in his conscience, in the nobility and magnanimity of his soul. Torturing animals to prolong human life has separated science form the most important thing that life has produced — the human conscience.

Powys, John Cowper, 1872-1963 (Welsh novelist and poet),
Morwyn

There seems to be no study too fragmented, no hypothesis too trivial...no design too warped, no methodology too bungled...no conclusions too trifling...for a paper to end up in print.

Rennie, Drummond, M.D. (*Journal of the American Medical Association* Deputy Editor), *JAMA*; 261: 2543-45, 1989

We will never know how unique we really are until we begin to act as humanly as we are able. Yet medical science, in looking forward to the day when it shall no longer be necessary for human beings to endure suffering, seems to believe more strongly than ever that inhumane methods are justifiable, for it is now engaged in an all-out attack upon pain itself. Experimental animals are being subjected to revoltingly painful investigations, because animal suffering is considered necessary to make human suffering unnecessary. Such a scientific outlook, I think typifies the objective humaneness of medical research in its failure to understand the basic issues at stake. These involve not so much the desirability of maintaining man in a state of perpetual good health as the desirability of his being able to attain a state of increased humanness.

Roberts, Dr. Catherine (Microbiologist), *The Scientific Conscience*, 1974

Rather than chronicle random cases that illustrate the pernicious nature of atheoretical research from a variety of scientific fields, it is perhaps better to focus upon the field most consistently guilty of mindless activity that results in great suffering. This is the field of experimental, behavioral, comparative, and sometimes physiological psychology. Nowhere are researchers further removed from theory, nowhere are researchers less engaged in trying to develop a picture of some aspect of the world, nowhere are researchers less able to discuss intelligently the significance of their experiments, nowhere are researchers less concerned with the morality of what they do.

Rollin, Bernard E. (Professor of Philosophy, Physiology and Biophysics, Colorado State University), *Animal Rights and Human Morality*, 1981

I believe that there should be restrictions on the use of human subjects in research, for example, and...that similar restrictions are appropriate in animal research.

Rowan, Andrew N., D.Phil. (Biochemist and former Director, Tufts Center for Animals and Public Policy), *Of Mice, Models & Men*, 1984

I would rather swear fifty lies than take an animal which had licked my hand in good fellowship and torture it.

Shaw, George Bernard, 1856-1950 (Nobel Prize-winning author), preface to *Doctor's Dilemma*

The distinction is not between useful and useless experiments, but between barbarous and civilized behaviour. Vivisection is a social evil because if it advances human knowledge, it does so at the expense of human character.

Ibid

Speciesism allows researchers to regard the animals they experiment on as items of equipment, laboratory tools rather than living, suffering creatures....This 'scientific' attitude to animals was exhibited to a large audience in December 1974 when the American public television network brought together Harvard philosopher Robert Nozick and three scientists whose work involves animals. The programme was a follow-up to Fred Wiseman's controversial film *Primate*, which had taken viewers inside the Yerkes Primate Center, a research centre in Atlanta, Georgia. Nozick asked the scientists whether the fact that an experiment will kill hundreds of animals is ever regarded, by scientists, as a reason for not performing it. One of the scientists answered: 'Not that I know of.' Nozick pressed his question: 'Don't the animals count at all?' Dr. A. Perachio, of the Yerkes Center, replied: 'Why should they?' While Dr. D. Baltimore, of the Massachusetts Institute of Technology, added that he did not think that experimenting on animals raised a moral issue at all. ("The Price of Knowledge" broadcast in New York, 12 December 1974.)

Singer, Peter, Ph.D. (Professor of Philosophy, Monash University, Australia), *Animal Liberation*, 1975

The extensive animal reproductive studies to which all new

drugs are now subjected are more in the nature of a public relations exercise than a serious contribution to drug safety. Animal tests can never predict the actions of drugs on humans.

Smithells, Professor R. W., in *Monitoring for Drug Safety*, 1980

It is not just that the weaker deserve the protection of the stronger. Nor is it just that other animals also feel pain or fear. Nor is it just that our behavior to other creatures reflects our own characters. Rather, we are shaped by what we do....What is the worth of medical miracles achieved at the cost of inflicting trauma on others that cannot help but scar our own characters?

Spaeth, George L., M.D. (Editor, *Ophthalmic Surgery*), editorial, July 1994, Vol. 25, No. 7

It is difficult to picture the great Creator conceiving of a programme of one creature (which He has made) using another living creature for purposes of experimentation. There must be other, less cruel ways of obtaining knowledge.

Stevenson, Adlai, 1900-1965 (U.S. political leader), *Putting First Things First*

In my judgement, we should lose nothing worth having by the abolition of vivisection, but were it otherwise, I am convinced that the promotion of justice, mercy and humanity among the human race would be well worth the sacrifice.

Thorton, Sir James Howard (Surgeon-General), *The Anti-Vivisection Review*, London, October 1910

What I think about vivisection is that if people admit that they have the right to take or endanger the life of living beings for the benefit of many, there will be no limit for their cruelty.

Tolstoy, Leo Nikolayevich, 1828-1910 (Russian novelist), letter, July 1909

My early career in animal research, like that of many scientists, shows a tragic irony. While artificially inducing aggression in coerced animals, I—not my subjects—was the true exemplar of human aggression. For many years, I tormented, injured, and killed laboratory rats, bred to be docile....What had reinforced my repeated mistreatment of innocent creatures? The pleasant sensations that accompany acceptance of grants, publication of papers, and presentation of guest lectures served as powerful reinforcers of my behavior.

Ulrich, Roger, Ph.D. (Psychologist), "Animal Research in Psychology: An Example of Reinforced Behavior", *Perspectives On Medical Research* 3: 49-53, 1991

When I finished my dissertation on pain-produced aggression, my Mennonite mother asked me what it was about. When I told her she replied, 'Well, we knew that. Dad always warned us to stay away from animals in pain because they are more likely to attack.' Today I look back with love and respect on all my animal friends from rats to monkeys who submitted to years of torture so that like my mother I can say, 'Well, we knew that.'

Ulrich, Roger, Ph.D. (Psychologist), letter, *American Psychological Association Monitor*, March 1978

It is totally unconscionable to subject defenseless animals to mutilation and death, just so a company can be the first to market a new shade of nail polish or a new, improved laundry detergent....It's cruel, it's brutal, it's inhumane, and most people don't want it.

Van Buren, Abigail, "Dear Abby," testifying before the House Judiciary Committee in support of the Consumer Products Safe Testing Act, March 1988

It is generally recognized that the traditional in vivo procedures were accepted without validation.

VanLooy, H. M., in *Alternatives to Animal Testing*, C.A. Reinhardt, ed., 1994

I am convinced the future of medical science does not hinge upon animal research, but rather on the development of more valid, reliable, efficient and innovative ways to advance medical knowledge....Ultimately our own inner peace and the very survival not only of other species on this earth but also of our own, will depend on our ability to foster an atmosphere of compassion for all life.

Wiebers, David O., M.D. (Professor of Neurology, Mayo Clinic), address to World Congress for Animals, June 1996

The most sweeping argument is that efforts to advance animal protection and human health are incompatible. Many exponents seek to reduce the situation to an us or them competition—human beings versus animals. The more fully articulated argument, advanced or implied by organisations and individuals within the medical community, is that any modification in animal use to enhance animal protection would undermine the future of medical science and thus threaten human health....This is not the case.

Wiebers, David O., M.D., Mayo Clinic, **Jennifer Leaning, M.D.**, Harvard Medical School, **Roger D. White, M.D.**, Mayo Clinic, "Animal protection and medical science," *The Lancet*, 343: 902-904, April 9, 1994

Society will be better off when the biomedical community recognises the animal-protection community as an extension of itself—allowing the alleviation of unnecessary suffering and death to extend to beings other than humans. Perhaps then we may realise the day when scientific investigators are moved to direct more of their efforts towards developing innovative and effective alternatives to animal use rather than innovative and effective ways to avoid changing the status quo.

Ibid

Experiments with animals have yielded considerable information concerning the teratogenic effects of drugs. Unfortunately, these experimental findings cannot be extrapolated from species to species or even from strain to strain within the same species, much less from animals to humans.

Yaffe, Professor S. J., University of Pennsylvania Department of Pediatrics and Pharmacology, *American College of Laboratory Animal Medicine*, p.13, 1980

That different countries use different LD50 [Lethal dose-50 percent] values for similar hazard categories only proves the

souls like ourselves

regulatory convenience and lack of real scientific merit [of the method].

Zbinden, Dr. Gerhard (Swiss toxicologist), quoted in Heidi J. Welsh, *Animal Testing and Consumer Products*, 1990

souls like ourselves

ACW 90

*T*aking into account that biology is the science of life, and that it is not coherent to base the teaching of such a science on the death of other beings...[and] giving priority to creation and not to destruction...the ministry resolves to ban vivisection and dissection of animals in all teaching establishments.

Argentine Ministry of Education and Justice, 1987

If every teacher and student considering dissection were to first witness the capture, handling and death of each animal they were about to dissect, dissection would fast become an endangered classroom exercise.

Balcombe, Jonathan P., Ph.D. (Ethologist), 1995

The student who refuses to participate in an activity which is or appears to be cruel should be encouraged, rather than discouraged. Compassion is far more difficult to teach than anatomy.

Barnard, Neal D., M.D. (Psychiatrist), 1995

Biological science curricula in which dissection of animals is required selects and has selected for a population of students who regard animals as disposable tools. This is probably why many biologists, biology educators, and health care professionals do not even think of considering using methods of teaching and research in which animals are not harmed.

Binkowski, Gloria J., V.M.D. (Veterinarian), 1995

It is unthinkable to me that...we continue to buy, pith, dissect and discard frogs and their body parts...in the name of science....We need a comprehensive environmental...attitude which includes all animals in their rightful place in the world. In my opinion their place is not the dissection table.

Bloom, Joyce, Ed.D. (Educator), 1995

In my experience, the sickest reptiles and amphibians I have ever seen have come from either fish markets or biological supply companies....The turtles I worked with from a biological supply company in the northeast were horribly ill with polysystemic disease, probably secondary to inadequate husbandry and chronic starvation.

Bonner, Barbara, D.V.M. (Veterinarian), 1995

By using models and discouraging inhumane and educationally pointless dissection, I feel I am encouraging my students to have a respect for all life, animal and human, that will extend beyond the boundaries of the classroom.

Boulton, Dennis R., M.S., 1987 Humane Educator of the Year, 1995

The often-used excuse that 'hands-on' experience is necessary for those wanting to become biologists or medical personnel simply is untrue. The experience of dissection is totally unnecessary for the biologically minded pre-college student.

Buyukmihci, Nedim C., V.M.D. (Veterinarian), 1995

To understand biology is to understand that all life is linked to the earth from which it came; it is to understand the stream of life, flowing out of the dim past into the uncertain future, is in reality a unified force, though composed of an infinite number and variety of separate lives. The essence of life is lived in freedom. Any concept of biology is not only sterile and profitless, it is distorted and untrue if it puts its primary focus on unnatural conditions rather than on those vast forces not of man's making, that shape and channel the nature and direction of life.

Carson, Rachel, 1907-1964 (Biologist and author), preface, *Humane Biology Projects*, 1977

In reality, the lack of respect for all living creatures shown by presenting dead [animals] for dissection probably deters more promising students from the 'life sciences' than it attracts.

Cliver, Suzanne, D.V.M. (Veterinarian), 1995

The cats [used for dissection] are mercilessly prodded, and jabbed, undoubtedly causing injuries to their eyes, heads and even potentially their internal organs. The hysteria in these cats, already caged inhumanely, and then jabbed with this lethal metal rod, is quite evident.

Ibid

I know of several biological supply houses in Louisiana and Mississippi which are notorious for finding a pond and collecting every living thing to be found within it....many of our states' ponds and bogs are devoid of herpetofauna because of this practice.

Crawford, Dez R. (Herpetologist), 1995

The suggestion that a surgeon is somehow better because he or she was trained on animals in medical school or in undergraduate biology or physiology or anatomy, let alone by dissection of frogs in high school, is totally unfounded.

Doyle, Donald E., M.D. (Surgeon), 1995

Year after year, animals are used to demonstrate the same well-known principles, although sophisticated models, videotapes, and computer simulations could easily substitute. These humane alternatives have many advantages, including reusability and durability.

Dunayer, Eric, V.M.D. (Veterinarian), 1995

In the end, science as we know it has two basic types of practitioners. One is the educated man who still has a controlled sense of wonder before the universal mystery, whether it hides in a snail's eye or within the light that impinges on that delicate organ. The second kind of observer is the extreme reductionist who is so busy stripping things apart that the tremendous mystery has been reduced to a trifle, to intangibles not worth troubling one's head about.

Eiseley, Loren (American environmental philosopher), *The Star Thrower*, 1978

It is inconsistent and improper to require a sincere student to perform dissections when, to that student, doing so violates her principles based on a reverence for all life.

Emmeluth, Donald, D.Ed. (Former president, National Association of Biology Teachers), 1995

It was concluded that the interactive videodisc-simulated lab [developed by the authors for studying the cardiovascular system] was as effective as the traditional live-animal labs and was more time efficient than the traditional participation lab.

Fawver, A. L., D.V.M., et al., *American Journal of Physiology*, 259: s11-s14, 1990

No valid educational system should seek, by coercion, conformity or tradition, to blunt students' sensitivity and force them to engage in activities that are contrary to their beliefs.

Fox, Michael W., D.Sc., Ph.D., B.Vet. Med. (Ethologist), 1995

The cause of education would not suffer if the classic dissection of frogs was removed from the high school curriculum.

Haddock, Nina J., Ph.D., M.Ed. (Clinical psychologist), 1995

The U.S. is suffering a crisis in science education. Those who say that stopping dissection in schools will damage the quality of education are at best naive. At worst, they are deliberately distracting us from the real problems such as illiteracy and innumeracy.

Hsu, Charles, Ph.D. (Geneticist), 1995

Better [instructional] methods exist and should be utilized to [stop] depletion of wild populations, such as crabs, sharks, and frogs.

Jenkins, Evelyn E., D.V.M. (Veterinarian), 1995

With physiology...I found the subject thoroughly repellent because of the vivisection, which was practiced merely for purposes of demonstration. I could never free myself from the feeling that warm-blooded creatures were akin to us and not just cerebral automata. Consequently I cut demonstration classes whenever I could.

Jung, Dr. Carl G., 1875-1961 (Swiss-German psychoanalyst), "Student Years," *Memories, Dreams, Reflections*, 1961

By now it is well known that a rat will sicken and die without certain foods and vitamins as it is that he will die if given no food at all. Would any one learn anything by poking out the eyes in order to prove that without them animals can't see?...Taught by such methods, biology not only fails to promote reverence for life, but encourages the tendency to blaspheme it. Instead of increasing empathy it destroys it. Instead of enlarging our sympathy it hardens the heart.

Krutch, Joseph Wood, 1893-1970 (American naturalist), *The Great Chain of Life*, 1956

Say what we will, there is a kind of moral deterioration inseparable from the act of killing anything which is doing us no harm....The beauty, the grace, the excellence of all harmless living things is the lesson for children, rather than precocious intimacy with the mystery of death.

Leffingwell, Albert, M.D., 1845-1916, editorial

Carving up a frog doesn't teach a student to think inquisitively; it teaches that living things are just commodities that can be bought and thrown out at the end of class.

Lockwood, Randall, Ph.D. (Ethologist), 1995

Computer-presented tutorial and simulation of biology laboratory concepts proved to be as good as or better than traditional approaches [that consume living or preserved animals] in increasing student academic performance.

More, D., M.S., and **C. L. Ralph, Ph.D.**, *Journal of Educational Technology Systems*, 1993

I do not believe that we can justify on moral or educational grounds the use of interventional experiments at the high school science fair level....It has taken me thirty years to reach my present state of awareness and I feel that I have only just begun. It is sad to have to admit that one's perception of the living world of which we are an integral part has been limited and impeded by a lack of knowledge unrelieved by a fairly extensive science education. I must reiterate that I believe that man's 'graspingness-of-mind' is a major part of his raison d'être. Whether he continues to evolve or perish depends to a great extent on the concept he has of life on this planet, including his own. High school biology education is the starting point of our human understanding of the integration of life as a whole and our place within it. We must ensure that it speaks of the oneness of all life first and its amazing complexity second.

Neil, David H. (Laboratory animal veterinarian), in *Animals in Education*, 1980

[Dissection] is on the decline—it is old fashioned. It is a responsibility of teachers to move with the times and keep up to date with what to teach. Since there are many good alternatives to dissection, a wise choice would be to use them.

Orlans, Barbara F., Ph.D. (Physiologist, Georgetown University), 1995

Undergraduate nursing and respiratory therapy students who [completed] an interactive video program on cardiac output principles [performed] significantly better on a learning post-test than a similar group completing a lecture and live-animal physiology laboratory.

Phelps, John L., Ph.D. (Health educator), 1995

I am convinced that biology should be taught as a course in human-animal relationships—not as a study of dead bodies or caged victims.

Richards, Dorothy, *Beaversprite: My Years Building an Animal Sanctuary*, 1977

I am often told that prospective physicians and veterinarians must 'get used to the sight of blood and death and to pain.' Yes, I reply, but must they get used to callously inflicting pain and causing death?...Surely sensitivity and good medicine are not mutually exclusive—indeed, are they not complementary?

Rollin, Bernard E. (Professor of Philosophy, Physiology and Biophysics, Colorado State University), *Animal Rights and Human Morality*, 1981

Looking back at the first half of my life as a zoologist, I am particularly impressed by one fact: none of the teachers, lecturers, or professors with whom I came into contact—and that includes my kindly father—none of the directors of laboratories where I worked, and none of my co-workers, ever discussed with me, or each other in my presence, the ethics of zoology. Nor did they ever ask me what I was really trying to do, what were my zoological aims and aspirations, and in what framework I saw the life-cycles I was elucidating. No one ever suggested that one should respect the lives of animals in the laboratory or that they, and not the experiments, however fascinating and instructive, were worthy of greater consideration....The fact is, teachers and pupils alike—quite aside from the question of earning their livings or furthering their careers as scientists—were brainwashed and self-indoctrinated. We were on the whole a rather moral group of seekers-after-truth, who loved the natural world and who were happily convinced of the importance of our subject—our research—but who were, lamentably, disinclined to think. It took me another thirty years of natural history and zoological laboratories before I, myself, began to consider the matter seriously and allowed my doubts to crystallize. This fortunate but traumatic experience I owe to my eldest daughter who, as a schoolgirl, resolutely marched out of her zoological classroom never to return. She refused to kill and then dissect an earthworm.

Rothschild, Miriam (Zoologist), *The Relationship between Animals and Man*, lecture, Oxford, England 1985

The psychological effects of vivisection and dissection and invasive animal experimentation on the personality of a young person cannot be overemphasized. In no way does vivisection or dissection make a young person better, more capable, or more humane.

Russell, George K., Ph.D. (Biologist), 1995

The power of science without the control of compassion and admiration for life is too immense to be applied merely for the satisfaction of scientific curiosity. If Biology were taught in a manner that developed a sense of wonder and of reverence for life, and if students felt inwardly enriched from their study of life, these students would formulate as a life-long goal the steadfast determination to protect and preserve all life and would bring healing to a world desperately in need of it.

Russell, George K., Ph.D. (Biologist), *American Biology Teacher*, 1972

I have worked with adolescents for more than ten years as a clinical psychologist and I can state categorically that the child's experience of dissection in schools, and his or her attitude towards it, can correlate with the child's whole attitude towards society. A child who has acquired a professional indifference to dissection is likely to a have a high score on the P scale of Eysenck's Personality Questionnaire—itself a feature of teenage delinquents and criminals....What are we doing when we brainwash children in schools to cut open their fellow animals? Are we dangerously desensitizing them? Some of the most warped and blunted people I know are those who have gone through prolonged trainings of this sort.

Ryder, Dr. Richard D. (Clinical psychologist), proceedings of the Human Education Council, Sussex University, 1980

Dissection can unintentionally foster fascination for gore and for further unsupervised experiments....Interactions with animals in school should foster respect for life via caring for animals and observing them in their natural environment, rather than dismemberment of an animal's body.

Schwartz, Sheila, Ed.D., United Federation of Teachers Humane Education Committee, 1995

Callousness and cruelty toward animals seems to be an expectation of the naive mind in laboratory studies involving animals....The children's experiments provide no cures for diseases or other useful advances; they simply cause pain and distress and set young minds off with a basic misconception of the meaning of research, a head start in insensitivity and an assumption that the strong may, with impunity, impose suffering and death on the weak.

Stevens, Christine, Animal Welfare Institute, in *Animals in Education*, 1980

The major reason given by students for liking this simulation [Interactive Frog Dissection] was their relief at not being required to dissect a frog.

Strauss, R. T., Ed.D., et al., *The American Biology Teacher*, 1991

The easy availability and nonchalant destruction of these beings desensitizes children to the underlying issues of cruelty and violence towards any life form.

Terrant, Suzanne C., D.V.M. (Veterinarian), 1995

There is no doubt these animals are, at best, severely stressed and terrified, at worst, inhumanely maimed and tortured....No living being should be subjected to such a cruel and inhumane death.

Ibid

I have just been through the process of killing the cistudo for the sake of science; but I cannot excuse myself for this murder, and see that such actions are inconsistent with the poetic perception, however they may serve science, and will alter the quality of my observations. I pray that I may walk more innocently and serenely through nature. No reasoning whatever reconciles me to this act. It affects my day injuriously. I have lost some self-respect. I have a murderer's experience to a degree.

Thoreau, Henry D., 1817-1862 (American poet and philosopher), *The Heart of Thoreau's Journals*

The capacity to perceive suffering in other beings and to respond with warmth and compassion is intertwined with scientific knowledge and skill in the complex endeavor we call the practice of medicine. For many years, animals have been used in the teaching of the science of medicine without considering its impact on the student's integration of compassion into the mix, and without taking sufficient stock of the perceptions and experience of the animals themselves.

Wiebers, D. O., M.D., Mayo Clinic, **R. A. Barron, M.D.**, Harvard Medical School, **J. Leaning, M.D.**, Harvard Medical School, **F. R. Ascione, Ph.D.**, Utah State University, "Ethics and animal issues in US medical education," *Medical Education*, 1994; 28

From the perspective of a physician involved in clinical practice, education and research, I have come to the conclusion that killing and dissecting animals is not only unnecessary but also counterproductive in the training of physicians and scientists.

Wiebers, David O., M.D. (Professor of Neurology, Mayo Clinic), 1995

The cavalier disregard exhibited towards the lives of...animals destined for our nation's schools and students is in stark contrast to the facade of white coats, gleaming scalpels and scientific principles espoused by the defenders of dissection as a pedagogical tool.

Zawistowski, Stephen, Ph.D. (Behavioral geneticist), 1995

souls like ourselves

8. ANIMAL CRUELTY AND HUMAN VIOLENCE

souls like ourselves

*W*e do not know how many batterers harm animals, nor, I would submit, do we need to quantify this form of battering to establish its import. It should be sufficient that those who work in battered women's shelters often know of batterers who threaten, harm, or murder animals or force sex between an animal and the woman....These workers have reported to me personally that cats are more likely to be stabbed or disemboweled, dogs to be shot, both may be hung, though a choke chain leash enables a batterer to act quickly against a dog; sometimes the pet simply disappears or dies mysteriously. Batterers have chopped off the heads or legs of cats, stepped on and thus killed a Chihuahua puppy. Cats have been found nailed to the front porch.

Adams, Carol J. (Writer), *Animals & Women*, 1995

I am sometimes asked: 'Why do you spend so much of your time and money talking about kindness to animals when there is so much cruelty to men?' I answer: 'I am working at the roots.'

Angell, George T., 1823-1909 (Founder of the Massachusetts Society for the Prevention of Cruelty to Animals), from a speech on February 14, 1884

Study after study show that all too often, people who abuse animals will abuse humans, too....If you see a beaten dog, suspect there might be an equally bruised elder. And if you find out an elder's being starved by their son or daughter, suspect the cat might be starving, too.

Ascione, Frank R., Ph.D. (Professor of Psychology, Utah State University), *Shepard's ElderCare/Law,* July, 1995

We must hammer home that love is indivisible. It is not 'either-or,' it is 'both-and,' because a society that cannot find the moral energy to care and act about gross animal suffering and exploitation will do little better about human need.

Baker, Reverend John Austin (Bishop of Salisbury [England]), sermon, October 4, 1986

You look at cruelty to animals and cruelty to humans as a continuum....This [animal cruelty] is not a harmless venting of emotion in a healthy individual; this is a warning sign that this individual...needs some sort of intervention....We try to tell people that investigating animal cruelty and investigating homicides may not be mutually exclusive.

Brantley, Alan (FBI Supervisory Special Agent), 1997

We cannot have peace among men whose hearts find delight in killing any living creature.

Carson, Rachel, 1907-1964 (Biologist and author), *Silent Spring*, 1962

As a society, we must realize that violent behavior rarely exists in a vacuum. We must recognize at-risk youths who lack empathy and compassion for animals and other human beings. It is our responsibility to do all that we can to teach these personality attributes to our youth so that today's animal abusers don't continue these despicable actions and become tomorrow's dangerous felons, thereby perpetuating the cycle of violence that has taken such a devastating toll on our society.

Cohen, Senator William, *Congressional Record*, May 2, 1996

Show me the enforced laws of a state for the prevention of cruelty to animals and I in turn will give you a correct estimate of the refinement, enlightenment, integrity and equity of that commonwealth's people....The lack of humane education is the principal cause of crime.

Dansheill, L. T., from a legislative address, Texas

If you have men who will exclude any of God's creatures from the shelter of compassion and pity, you will have men who will deal likewise with their fellow men.

Francis of Assisi, Saint, 1181-1226, quoted in *Life* by St. Bonaventura

Nothing so endangers the fineness of the human heart as the possession of power over others; nothing so corrodes it as the callous or cruel exercise of that power; and the more helpless the creature over whom the power is cruelly or callously exercised, the more the human heart is corroded.

Galsworthy, John, 1867-1933 (Nobel Prize-winning novelist)

I hold that, the more helpless a creature, the more entitled it is to protection by man from the cruelty of man.

Gandhi, Mohandas Karamchand, 1869-1948, The Mahatma (Great Soul), *An Autobiography, The Story of My Experiments*

I hope to make people realize how totally helpless animals are, how dependent on us, trusting as a child must that we will be kind and take care of their needs....[They] are an obligation put on us, a responsibility we have no right to neglect, nor to violate by cruelty.

Herriot, James, 1916-1995 (English veterinarian and author), in a television interview

Cruelty to animals is the degrading attitude of paganism.

Hinsley, Cardinal, 1865-1943 (Fifth archbishop of Westminster)

As we prepare to enter a new millennium, we are faced with a very different kind of environmental concern, one that promises a different type of 'silent spring'—the proliferation of violence in our society. Every day we hear stories of innocent voices, including those of both children and animals, silenced by unspeakable acts of abuse and cruelty. Increasingly, these acts are the work of perpetrators who are children themselves. A 1995 *Time* magazine essay on violence in Middle America entitled 'Johnny Got a Gun' describes the crimes committed by a group of adolescents in Omaha, Nebraska, who began their violent spree by shooting many of the songbirds in their community. This new silent spring will require a response as wide-reaching as the environmental activism of the past.

Irwin, Paul G. (President, The Humane Society of the United States), 1998

If [man] is not to stifle his human feelings, he must practise kindness towards animals, for he who is cruel to animals becomes hard also in his dealings with men. We can judge the heart of a man by his treatment of animals.

Kant, Immanuel, 1724-1804 (German philosopher), *Lectures on Ethics*

This paper has reviewed a number of results from a study of childhood cruelty toward animals, motivations for animal cruelty, and family violence. The strength of these findings suggests that aggression among adult criminals may be strongly correlated with a history of family abuse and childhood cruelty toward animals....[These] data should alert researchers, clinicians, and societal leaders to the importance of childhood cruelty as a potential indicator of disturbed family relationships and future antisocial and aggressive behavior. The evolution of a more gentle and benign relationship in human society might be enhanced by our promotion of a more positive and nurturing ethic between children and animals.

Kellert, Stephen R., Ph.D., Yale University and **Alan R. Felthous, M.D.**, University of Texas, "Childhood Cruelty toward Animals among Criminals and Noncriminals," *Human Relations* 38: 1113-29, 1985

Animal abusers are five times more likely than their peers to commit violent crimes against human beings. They're four times more likely to commit property offenses, three times more likely to be drug offenders. We have to take this seriously because it gives us an indication that—that these people who commit animal abuse may also abuse human beings.

Levin, Dr. Jack (Professor of Sociology, Northeastern University), interview, January 15, 1998

This tendency [to cruelty] should be watched in them [children], and, if they incline to any such cruelty, they should be taught contrary usage. For the custom of tormenting and killing other animals will, by degrees, harden their hearts even towards men.

Locke, John, 1632-1704 (English philosopher), *Thoughts on Education*

Animal abuse by any member of the family, whether parent or child, often means child abuse is going on too.

Lockwood, Randall, Ph.D. (Ethologist), 1997

We strongly believe that the wounds in human relationships and human-animal relationships are preventable and that empathy and compassion for all fellow creatures, human and nonhuman, must be nurtured and sustained. We hope that by highlighting the connections between cruelty to animals and interpersonal violence, the potential for violence in all its forms will be reduced.

Lockwood, Randall, Ph.D. (Ethologist) and **Frank R. Ascione, Ph.D.** (Psychologist), *Cruelty to Animals and Interpersonal Violence*, 1998

Cruelty has cursed the human family for countless ages. It is almost impossible for one to be cruel to animals and kind to humans. If children are permitted to be cruel to their pets and other animals, they easily learn to get the same pleasure from the misery of fellow-humans. Such tendencies can easily lead to crime.

McGrand, Fred A., parliamentary address, Ottawa, Canada

One of the most dangerous things that can happen to a child is to kill or torture an animal and get away with it.

Mead, Margaret, Ph.D., 1901-1978 (American anthropologist)

In many parts of the present day world of great mobility...the tabus about killing and torturing living creatures are no longer reliable....It would, therefore, seem wise to include a more carefully planned handling of behavior toward living creatures in our school curriculum....

Mead, Margaret, Ph.D., 1901-1978 (American anthropologist), Midcontinent Psychiatric Meeting, September 14, 1963

The indifference, callousness and contempt that so many people exhibit toward animals is evil first because it results in great suffering in animals, and second because it results in an incalculably great impoverishment of human spirit.

Montagu, Dr. Ashley (British-American anthropologist), *Of Man, Animals and Morals*

souls like ourselves

It is dishonourable to break a contract and that is what we have done with our animal friends. They are our relatives and we too are animals. To be brutal to them is to become brutalised in all our dealings, with humans as well as with other species. Any culture that knows sympathy for its animal companions will be a culture that is sensitive and caring in all respects. Any culture that feels a kinship with animals will be a culture that keeps faith with its roots....If we forget our humble origins we will soon start to imagine that we can do what we like with our little planet. Before too long we will become the new dinosaurs, fossils of some future age.

Morris, Dr. Desmond (English author and animal behaviorist), *The Animal Contract*, 1991

What should we think of a stout and strong man, that should exert his fury and barbarity on a helpless and innocent babe? Should we not abhor and detest that man, as a mean, cowardly, and savage wretch, unworthy [of] the stature and strength of a man? No less mean, cowardly, and savage is it, to abuse and torment the innocent beast, who can neither help himself nor avenge himself; and yet has as much right to happiness in this world as a child can have: nay, more right, if this world be his only inheritance.

Primatt, Humphrey, D.D., 18th century (English Christian Doctor of Divinity), *A Dissertation on the Duty of Mercy and Sin of Cruelty to Brute Animals*

As long as man continues to be the ruthless destroyer of lower living beings, he will never know health or peace. For as long as men massacre animals, they will kill each other. Indeed, he who sows the seed of murder and pain cannot reap joy and love.

Pythagoras, 6th century B.C. (Greek philosopher and mathematician), depicted in Ovid: *The Metamorphoses*

Many have held up usefulness to human beings as the sole criterion for the evaluation of an animal's life. Upon closer examination, one discovers that this mode of evaluation of another's life and right to existence has also been responsible for human indifference as well as cruelty to animals, not to speak of violence in today's world....On sober reflection, one can find that there is a striking similarity between exterminating the life of a wild animal for fun, and terminating the life of an innocent fellow human being at the whim of a more capable and powerful person....We should therefore be wary of justifying the right of any species to survive solely on the basis of its usefulness to human beings.

Rinpoche, Nomgyal, "The Buddhist Declaration on Nature"

Cases of animal cruelty by children can no longer be dismissed as 'boys will be boys' or 'it's just a phase.' Violence wreaked on animals by adults should no longer be viewed as an isolated incident, but a warning that the humans in the family may be at risk or even already abused....We must, as prosecutors, recognize that it is unacceptable to excuse and ignore acts of cruelty toward animals. Anyone who can commit such cruelty is in desperate need of incarceration, counseling or other immediate intervention. We cannot afford to accept such violence, nor will the public let us.

Ritter, William A., Jr. (District Attorney), "The cycle of violence often begins with violence toward animals," *The Prosecutor*, 30: 31-33, 1996

Just as we have to depersonalize human opponents in wartime in order to kill them with indifference, so we have to create a void between ourselves and the animals on which we inflict pain and misery for profit.

Rothschild, Miriam (Zoologist), *The Relationship between Animals and Man*, lecture, Oxford, England 1985

When I see a person indifferent to the needs and blind to the sufferings of animals, I put him down as one from whom little sympathy can be expected for the needs and sufferings of his neighbours.

Ruskin, John, 1819-1900 (British philosopher and artist), speech at Oxford, England, December 9, 1884

The cause of each and all of the evils that afflict the world is the same—the general lack of humanity, the lack of the knowledge that all sentient life is akin, and that he who injures a fellow being is in fact doing injury to himself.

Salt, Henry, 1851-1939 (English scholar and writer), *Seventy Years Among Savages*

When we turn to the protection of animals, we sometimes hear it said that we ought to help men first and animals afterwards. But if the principle which prompts the humane treatment of men is the same essentially as that which prompts the humane treatment of animals, how can we successfully safeguard it in one direction while we violate it in another? By condoning cruelty to animals we perpetuate the very spirit which condones cruelty to men.

> **Salt, Henry**, 1851-1939 (English scholar and writer), *The Encyclopaedia of Religion and Ethics*

Anyone who has accustomed himself to regard the life of any living creature as worthless is in danger of arriving also at the idea of worthless human lives.

> **Schweitzer, Albert, Ph.D., M.D.**, 1875-1965 (Nobel Peace Prize-winning humanitarian)

Very little of the great cruelty shown by men can really be attributed to cruel instinct. Most of it comes from thoughtlessness or inherited habit. The roots of cruelty, therefore, are not so much strong as widespread. But the time must come when inhumanity protected by custom and thoughtlessness will succumb before humanity championed by thought. Let us work that this time may come.

> **Schweitzer, Albert, Ph.D., M.D.**, 1875-1965 (Nobel Peace Prize-winning humanitarian), *Memoirs of Childhood and Youth*, 1949

Man is distinctly more aggressive, cruel, and relentless than any of the other apes.

> **Spock, Benjamin, M.D.**, 1904-1998 (Pediatrician and author), *Decent and Indecent*, 1970

Childhood animal abuse is but a single strand on the web of generalized societal violence against animals and people. It starts in your own house and it will come home to haunt you unless we, as a society, become vigilant to always instill in ourselves and the ones we love a respect and consideration for the rest of life.

> **Stoller, Kenneth P., M.D.** (Pediatrician), 1989

The National Rifle Association would be proud. It spent over $83 million last year to insure that families...could train their children how to own, handle and fire guns properly. Educators take heed. After having hands-on experience in killing defenseless woodland creatures, coupled with mind-numbing Nintendo-type video assassination games, real murder is only a merit badge away.

Ibid

The case histories of delinquents of brutal and homicidal tendencies often reveal that cruelties and brutalities were first performed on dogs, cats or other animals....This spiritual universe is responsive to feelings rather than intellect. The unfeeling man, no matter how brilliant, is a thoroughly sick soul. And I submit that in education of children and adolescent youth, nothing should enter the curriculum that tends to produce unfeeling callousness.

Thompson, Dorothy, 1894-1961 (Journalist and syndicated columnist), interview, February 1960

9. THE ENVIRONMENT AND NATURAL WORLD

To enter the genetic structure of any being is to enter into its most sacred and most intimate reality....The claim for 'betterment' is consistently driven by a certain arrogance that we can observe in the commitment of modern society to taking over control of life processes by manipulative procedures. The very evils that we propose to cure in humans by genetic engineering are themselves frequently caused by prior industrial engineering of the planet. It should be clear by now that we have neither the intelligence nor the discipline required for any general or long-term beneficial improvement upon what nature is doing at the deeper level of its functioning.

Berry, Father Thomas (Catholic priest and writer), *Earth Ethics*, Fall 1994

If the earth does grow inhospitable toward human presence, it is primarily because we have lost our sense of courtesy toward the earth and its inhabitants, our sense of gratitude, our willingness to recognize the sacred character of habitat, our capacity for the awesome, for the numinous quality of every earthly reality.

Berry, Father Thomas (Catholic priest and writer), *The Dream of the Earth*, 1988

Hurt not the earth, neither the sea, nor the trees.

Bible, The, Revelation 7:3

If we are to teach children how to respect their human and natural environment and all its elements they must be taught they are a part of nature: 'All life is one and all its manifestations are ascending the ladder of evolution.' One of the objectives of education from nursery school onwards must be to give children a balanced sensitivity to life—a humane education.

Canadian Senate Committee on Health, Welfare and Science, report, *Child at Risk*

As cruel a weapon as the cave man's club, the chemical barrage has been hurled against the fabric of life.

Carson, Rachel, 1907-1964 (Biologist and author), *Silent Spring*, 1962

The 'control of nature' is a phrase conceived in arrogance, born of the Neanderthal age of biology and philosophy, when it was supposed that nature exists for the convenience of man.

Ibid

Viewed ecologically, the human saga is a tragic success story.

Catton, William R., Jr. (Author), *Deep Ecology*, 1985

Sooner or later, wittingly or unwittingly, we must pay for every intrusion on the natural environment.

Commoner, Barry (Biologist and educator), *Science and Survival*, 1966

It shall be the fundamental duty of every citizen of India to protect and improve the Natural Environment including forests, lakes, rivers and wildlife, and to have compassion for all living creatures.

Constitution of India, Article 51-A [g]

The monumental problem for the future is [human] over-population.

Cousteau, Jacques-Yves, 1910-1997 (French oceanographer), 1996

Saving marshlands and redwoods does not need biological justification any more than does opposing callousness and vandalism. The cult of wilderness is not a luxury; it is a necessity....

Dubos, René, Ph.D., 1901-1982 (Microbiologist), *A God Within*, 1972

Human numbers and human behavior must be brought into line with the constraints placed upon Homo Sapiens by the limits of Earth and the laws of nature. People who think those can be ignored or evaded are living in a dream world. They haven't reflected on the four million years it took for humanity to build a population of two billion people, in contrast to the forty-five years in which the second two billion appeared and the twenty-two years it will take for the arrival of the third two billion. They have overlooked the most important trend of their time.

> **Ehrlich, Dr. Paul** (Professor of Population Studies and Professor of Biological Sciences, Stanford University), *The Population Explosion*, 1990

Mother Earth is in jeopardy, caused by the anthropocentrism of religion, education, and science during the past three centuries. A new beginning is required, centered on the *sacredness of the planet*.

> **Fox, Matthew** (Episcopalian priest and visionary author), "My Final Statement Before Being Silenced by the Vatican," 1989

Some proponents say genetic engineering is merely an extension of natural selective breeding through traditional practices....I don't see transgenic research as a natural extension—there is nothing natural about it. It is an intensification of our manipulation of nonhuman life forms.

> **Fox, Michael W., D.Sc., Ph.D., B.Vet.Med.** (Ethologist), 1994

The maltreatment of the natural world and its impoverishment leads to the impoverishment of the human soul. It is related to the outburst of violence in human society. To save the natural world today means to save what is human in humanity.

> **Gorbachev, Raisa M.,** *I Hope*, 1991

We each need to assess our own relationship to the natural world and renew, at the deepest level of personal integrity, a connection to it.

> **Gore, Al** (Vice President of the United States), *Earth in the Balance*, 1992

souls like ourselves

To heal the Earth, we must also heal ourselves. The environment is not something "out there." There are no boundaries between ourselves and our environment. We eat our environment. We drink it. We breathe it. The Earth flows through us, as well as around us. We can have no respect for ourselves if we do not also respect the Earth.

Hayes, Denis (American environmentalist and National Coordinator of the first Earth Day), speech on the Mall, Washington D.C., Earth Day 1990

Whether you are buying a car or casting a ballot, choosing a job or planning a family, follow your moral compass. Don't let others define you. Don't let advertisers mold you; don't let zealots ensnare you; don't let conventional wisdom trap you. Remember you are part of a much larger whole. Glean the wisdom offered by 3,000-year-old bristlecone pines. Listen to the elegiac verse of the humpback whales. Contemplate the choices between smart bombs and smart kids, between global warming and a sustainable future, between gluttony and balance.

Ibid

People are often heard to say that they are concerned about the kind of world we will leave to our grandchildren, and I am one of them. But I am equally concerned about the kind of grandchildren we shall leave to the earth.

Hoyt, John A. (President Emeritus, The Humane Society of the United States), speech, July 16, 1996

It was first of all necessary to civilize man in relation to his fellow men. That task is already well advanced and makes progress daily. But it is also necessary to civilize man in relation to nature. There, everything remains to be done....In the relations of man with the animals, with the flowers, with all the objects of creation, there is a whole great ethic [*toute une grande morale*] scarcely seen as yet, but which will eventually break into the light and be the corollary and the complement to human ethics.

Hugo, Victor, 1802-1885 (French poet and novelist), *Alps et Pyrénées*

Sit down before fact like a little child, and be prepared to give up every preconceived notion, follow humbly wherever and to whatever abyss Nature leads, or you shall learn nothing.

Huxley, T. H., 1825-1895 (English biologist)

The alteration, through genetic engineering, of the permanent genetic code of animals represents a unique and unprecedented assault on their dignity and biological integrity....If we continue over the next decades to mix and match the genes of the animal kingdom to suit our desires and to gain commercial profits, it could bring about the end of nature as we have known it.

Kimbrell, Andrew (Lawyer and social reformer), *The Human Body Shop: The Engineering and Marketing of Life*, 1994

We never seem to have a feeling for all living things on the earth. If we could establish a deep abiding relationship with nature we would never kill an animal for our appetite, we would never harm, vivisect, a monkey, a dog, a guinea pig for our benefit. We would find other ways to heal our wounds, heal our bodies. But the healing of the mind is something totally different. That healing gradually takes place if you are with nature, with that orange on the tree, and the blade of grass that pushes through the cement, and the hills covered, hidden, by the clouds.

Krishnamurti, Jiddu, 1895-1986 (Indian philosopher and spiritual teacher), *Krishnamurti to Himself: His Last Journal*, 1987

The cockroach and the birds were both here long before we were. Both could get along very well without us, although it is perhaps significant that of the two the cockroach would miss us more.

Krutch, Joseph Wood, 1893-1970 (American naturalist), *The Twelve Seasons*, 1949

Over the centuries it has proved convenient for us to assert that we are valuable because we are human. But simply to assert the in-itself value of the natural world may not prove sufficient to withstand the press of technology, population pressure, economic expansion and sheer human bloody-mindedness....Eventually, and better sooner than later, we must learn how to discern the contours of our own nest, and in cleaning it up, save the nests of all other species as well as our own.

Leaning, Jennifer, M.D., *Harvard Medical*, Vol. 64, No. 1, Summer 1990

Moral education, as I understand it, is not about inculcating obedience to law or cultivating self-virtue, it is rather about finding within us an ever-increasing sense of the worth of creation. It is about how we can develop and deepen our intuitive sense of beauty and creativity.

Linzey, Reverend Dr. Andrew, Center for the Study of Theology, University of Essex, U.K, proceedings of the Humane Education Council at Sussex University, 1980

The meat-eating quarter of humanity poses enormous demands on the world's environment. Forty percent of the world's grain production is required to feed and fatten the livestock...good quality land can yield up to ten times more protein if used to grow crops than if used to graze cattle.

McMichael, A. J. (Professor, Department of Community Medicine, University of Adelaide, South Australia), *Planetary Overload*, 1993

Just how many people can the world feed, clothe and shelter, on an ongoing basis? Unlike other species, humans can deliberately and artificially extend the sustainable productivity base of their environment. This can only be done at the expense of other species, by commandeering natural habitat for human purposes.

Ibid

Every animal that walks the earth, or swims, or flies is precious beyond description, something so rare and wonderful that it equals the stars or the ocean or the mind of man. Animals form an inalienable fragment of nature, and if we hasten the disappearance of even one species, we diminish our world and our place in it.

Michener, James, 1907-1997 (U.S. novelist), 1976

Any home can be made uninhabitable. Our culture has too often talked in terms of *conquering* nature. This is about as sensible as for a caddis worm to think of conquering the pond that supports it, or a drunk to start fighting the bed he is lying on. Our dignity arises *within* nature, not against it.

Midgley, Mary (Former Senior Lecturer in Philosophy, University of Newcastle-upon-Tyne, U.K.), *Beast and Man*, 1978

The forests of America, however slighted by man, must have been a great delight to God, because they were the best He ever planted.

Muir, John, 1838-1914 (Scottish/American naturalist), in John Gunther, *Inside U.S.A.*, 1947

Everybody needs beauty as well as bread, places to play in and pray in, where Nature may heal and cheer and give strength to body and soul alike.

Muir, John, 1838-1914 (Scottish/American naturalist), *The Yosemite*, 1912

When we try to pick out anything by itself, we find it hitched to everything else in the universe.

Muir, John, 1838-1914 (Scottish/American naturalist), 1911

Animals do not tell us to be happy, never demand that we dwell in nature. Rather, often in their presence, we are happy, we do dwell in nature. On one level, their great gift falls away as nothing more than our permitting them to act as benefactors. But there is nothing matter-of-fact about this gift. The gift given by animals is precious: a guide back to balance. On that level the gift is the basis of a profound mystery.

Nollman, Jim (Musician and author), *Animal Dreaming*, 1987

Among political ecologists especially one sometimes encounters the idea that non-human nature, including animals, is out there passively waiting for us to construct it materially and conceptually and give meaning to it. It is implied that our concept of nature is the only thing real and that it is therefore up to us humans to decide what we want nature to be. Such a view totally overlooks the possible existence of other realities apart from the human one, and the meanings that animals impose upon their world, a world which may or may not include us!

Noske, Barbara (Anthropologist), *Humans and Other Animals*, 1989

In the end we must, I think, somehow conclude that they [the animals] have as much right to this planet as we have.

Philip, Prince (Duke of Edinburgh), speech, New York, 1971

Greater separation from nature makes it easier and easier to capture, maim and kill with impunity. Seeing the vague outline from afar is not the same as hearing the breath rush in and out of the nostrils. The desacralization process allows human beings to repudiate the intimate relationship and likeness that exist between ourselves and all other things that live.

Rifkin, Jeremy (Author), *Algeny*, 1983

It is hard to conceive how much we have environmentally to gain by switching to a more vegetarian diet. There is not a single aspect of the ecological crisis that would not be immediately and profoundly improved by such a transformation.

Robbins, John (Author), in *Sustainable Development*, a publication of Global Tomorrow Coalition, 1990

Even the best of the animal enterprises examined returns only 34.5% of the investment of fossil energy to us in food energy, whereas the poorest of five crop enterprises examined returns 328%.

Roller, W. L. et al., "Energy Costs of Intensive Livestock Production," American Society of Agricultural Engineers, June, 1975, St. Joseph, Michigan

Save the birds: save the world. It has become as simple as that, because lasting conservation of the world's birds can only be achieved if we take action to protect and conserve the ecological health of the whole planet. So simple, yet so hard....Perhaps we can start by taking a lesson from the birds themselves. They acknowledge no borders. It is a principle we should make our own.

Schreiber, Rudolpf L. (Publisher and conservationist), *Save the Birds*, 1989

Whatever befalls the earth befalls the sons of the earth. Man did not weave the web of life, he is merely a strand of it. Whatever he does to the web, he does to himself.

Seattle, Chief, 1786-1866 (Native American leader), an 1854 oration

In the ancient spiritual traditions, man was looked upon as part of nature, linked by indissoluble spiritual and psychological bonds with the elements around him....What is needed today is to remind ourselves that nature cannot be destroyed without humankind ultimately being destroyed itself....Let us recall the ancient Hindu dictum: 'The Earth is our mother, and we are all her children.'

Singh, Dr. Karan, "The Hindu Declaration on Nature," September 1986

We travel together, passengers on a little spaceship, dependent on its vulnerable reserves of air and soil; all committed for our safety to its security and peace; preserved from annihilation only by the care, the work and, I will say, the love we give our fragile craft.

Stevenson, Adlai E.,1900-1965 (U.S. political leader), in *Exploring New Ethics for Survival*, 1972

The real lesson of the future is that it will be what we make it. Our actions—or inaction—will be decisive. We are now in command of our own evolution. The choices we make individually and collectively will provide the ultimate answer to our destiny.

Strong, Maurice (Former Director, Environmental Program of the United Nations)

Part of what justice means for nonhuman animals is that there will just have to be fewer people, because I think the insistence of people to cover the Earth is itself a grievous insult to the nonhuman animals whose space is squeezed into nonexistence. Just because people can have three, four, and five children does not mean that that's the best thing for all creation. It definitely is not.

Walker, Alice (Pulitzer Prize-winning author), interview, April 1988

As an instrument of planetary home repair, it is hard to imagine anything as safe as a tree.

Weiner, Jonathan (Former writer/editor for *The Sciences*), *The Next One Hundred Years*, 1990

Humankind has been increasingly moving away from nature, perverting, degrading and destroying its substances and processes and living things. Genetic engineering is a moving away. Now the movement must be toward, if nature is to be preserved, if the life and beauty of this planet are to be preserved.

Welborn, Robert (Attorney and humanitarian), 1994

When the century began, neither human numbers nor technology had the power radically to alter planetary systems. As the century closes, not only do vastly increased human numbers and their activities have that power, but major, unintended changes are occurring in the atmosphere, in soils, in waters, among plants and animals, and in the relationships among all of these. The rate of change is out-stripping the ability of scientific disciplines and our current capabilities to assess and advise. It is frustrating the attempts of political and economic institutions, which evolved in a different, more fragmented world, to adapt and cope.

World Commission on Environment and Development, *Our Common Future*, 1987

souls like ourselves

10. HUNTING AND FISHING

too was once a sportsman. But I grew up.

Abbey, Edward (American essayist and author), The Journey
Home: *Some Words in Defense of the American West*, 1991

I saw one doe, her right shoulder arrowed and swollen, still
leading her half-grown fawn.

Anonymous eyewitness to Kentucky's Lexington-Bluegrass
Army Depot bow hunt, quoted in *Mankind?*, 1974

The panic of the animals, huddled together, with their rolling
eyes and slavering tongues made for me an unforgettable
sight. They made no sound. The only noise was the howling
of the jerks pumping arrows into them.

Anonymous eyewitness to Ohio's Ravenna Arsenal public bow
hunt, quoted in *Mankind?*, 1974

One man is proud when he has caught a poor hare, and
another when he has taken a little fish in a net, and another
when he has taken wild boars, and another when he has taken
bears....Are not these robbers?

Aurelius, Marcus (Antoninus), 121-180 (Roman philosopher),
Meditations

If father kicks the cat, then cat-kicking becomes the right
thing to do in the eyes of the toddler. He is wide open to influ-
ences of every kind and will see no inconsistency in the fact
that father is kind—let us say—to dogs....I do not suggest that
all hunting people are hard-hearted in their dealings with their
fellow-men, but the danger is that when once we have exclud-

ed a group of human beings or animals as being undeserving of sympathy we have started 'compartmental thinking,' by which one set of values can be walled off from the criticism applied to another by personal conscience and community opinion.

Barter, Gwendolen, from "Children and Hunting," in *Against Hunting, a Symposium*, Patrick Moore (ed.)

And in that day, will I make a covenant for them with the beasts of the field, and with the fowls of heaven, and with the creeping things of the ground; and I will break the bow and the sword, and the battle out of the earth; and I will make them to lie down safely.

Bible, The, Hosea 2:18-20

I grew up around guns. You know, hunting guns. I used to be a hunter....But I'm not a hunter now. I'm getting older, and I guess I'm mellowed out. I just don't want to kill anything anymore.

Bird, Larry (Professional basketball player and coach), interview, 1997

Guns, hunting dogs primed for blood, the crisp air of autumn mornings, the camaraderie of all-male companions...these constituted a rite of passage from boyhood into manhood in my native Ozark mountains. I loved the smell of the trees, the feel of the ridges and valleys. The excitement of the hunt—'buck fever'—was a welcome relief from a life lived within walls and towns....Yet the actual killing disturbed me. The hardest part was 'finishing off' a downed animal, bleeding from bullet wounds, exhausted from the chase, facing death. Try as I might, I could neither ignore nor forget the fearful look in those pleading eyes. In this way I learned that every creature values her or his life just as much as I value mine. Although I continued to hunt for a time, I was already a dormant, would-be vegetarian, lacking sufficient moral courage—and nutritional information—to act on my most fundamental feelings and intuitions.

Boyd, Billy Ray (Author), *For the Vegetarian in You*, 1996

The animal welfare and rights movement must extend its

influence into the area of conservation. For too long we have allowed the conservation bodies to exist without the ethic of 'rights for the individual,' with the result that many blood-sportsmen have been allowed to mask their cruel activities by wearing the respectable mantles of 'conservation' simply because they take action to preserve their victims and their habitats.

Bryant, John M. (English engineer and author), *Fettered Kingdoms*, 1982

To make sport of taking life, to do it for fun, to organize it into a form of collective enjoyment, is to fail to act responsibly and with a proper reverence for God's creation.

Carpenter, Edward (Dean of Westminster), in *Against Hunting, a Symposium*, Patrick Moore (ed.)

It is time everyone knew something that it took me forty years to learn—that all hunting for 'sport,' and fox-hunting above all, is organized torture leading to murder....The lesson has been a painful one to me.

Churchward, Robert, 1907-1981, *A Master of Hounds Speaks*

What pleasure can it possibly be to a man of culture, when either a puny human being is mangled by a most powerful beast, or a splendid beast is transfixed with a hunting spear?

Cicero, Marcus Tullius, 106-43 B.C. (Roman scholar and writer), *Letter to Friends 7.1*

The law sends a carter to prison who, for his living, drives a horse with a sore neck to market, but has nothing to say against the nobility, clergy, and others who, for their amusement, hunt a stag for seven hours and more, inflicting unspeakable anguish upon it, ending in an awful death.

Coleridge, Stephen, 1854-1936 (British reformer), *Vivisection: A Heartless Science*

I have myself been the unwilling witness of an otter hunt, and a more sickening spectacle it is difficult to conceive. That any man or woman, much less than any Christian, could be possessed with so much cruelty and cowardice, and could derive pleasure from such a pitiful scene of hopeless suffering, filled me with unutterable disgust.

Ibid

The arrow went through the doe's neck. We all saw it strike, and we all saw it sticking out of both sides as she bounded away. We came to several pools of blood with prints of her knees beside them where she had gone down to hang her head and bleed in the bright sun. We saw spots where she had stumbled. But still her life's blood ran, and still she went on. At last we found her, and she was dying. She was on her knees and hocks. Her ears, no longer the wonderful alert warning system, were sagging. Her head was down, her nose was in her blood. Somehow, the doe lurched up. Stumbling, bounding, crashing blindly into the brush, she managed to reach the rim of the plateau we were on and disappear. We fanned out and combed the hillside. We failed. I vowed never to hunt with a bow again.

Conley, Clint (Ex-Class A archer), 1991

If any member of my family considered it 'great fun' to watch an animal be torn to pieces, I'd send him to the nearest shrink.

Cromie, Bob (*Chicago Tribune* columnist), quoted in *Mankind?*, 1974, responding to a statement by the National Beagle Club president that beagling and fox hunting is great family fun

The confession of one who for years hunted and killed before he learned that the wild offered a more thrilling sport than slaughter—and the hope that what I have written may make others feel and understand that the greatest thrill of the hunt is not in killing, but in letting live.

Curwood, James Oliver, 1878-1927 (Author), introduction, *The Grizzly King*, 1916

You ask people why they have deer heads on the wall. They always say, 'Because it's such a beautiful animal.' There you go. I think my mother's attractive, but I have photographs of her.

DeGeneres, Ellen (Comedian), "On Location: Women of the Night"

The hunter knows the excitement of stalking and the excitement of the kill. Yet in time he often comes to realize that satisfaction of his atavistic desire serves an ignoble end and that preservation of wildlife ranks higher.

Douglas, William O., 1898-1980 (U.S. Supreme Court Justice),
A Wilderness Bill of Rights

Then I went through a shooting and fishing phase, a black period in my relations to nature, and one which now, taught by Clare and Thoreau, I look back on with an angry shame.

Fowles, John (British novelist), 1971

[On the regret he felt for killing an antelope on a hunting trip] First: had I not been there that day, he would be standing now in the Wyoming snow, drifted down the sage, his does and fawns around him. Second: I will never again interfere in the lives of my fellow creatures.

Gilligan, Edmund (Former outdoor sports columnist for the *New York Herald Tribune*), interview, 1962

Who can dispute the inhumanity of the sport of hunting—of pursuing a poor defenceless creature for mere amusement, till it becomes exhausted by terror and fatigue, and of then causing it to be torn to pieces by a pack of dogs? From what kind of instruction can men, and even women, imbibe such principles as these? And what can their pleasure in it consist of? Is it not solely in the agony they produce to the animal? They will pretend it is not and try to make us believe so too— that it is merely in the pursuit. But what is the object of their pursuit? Is there any other than to torment and destroy?

Gompertz, Lewis, 1779-1861 (British humanitarian and founder of the Royal Society for the Prevention of Cruelty to Animals)
Moral Inquiries on the Situation of Man and of Brutes, 1824

We clearly rank the practice of hunting and shooting for diversion, with vain sports; and we believe the awakened mind may see that even the leisure of those whom Providence hath permitted to have a competence for world-ly goods, is but ill filled up with these amusements. Therefore, being not only accountable for our substance, but also for our time, let our leisure be employed in serving our neighbour and not in distressing the creatures of God for our amusement.

Gurney, Joseph John, 1788-1847, *Observations*

More than 90 percent of the public does not hunt, and recent poll results (*Los Angeles Times* 1993, Associated Press 1995) indicate that a majority of Americans oppose recreational killing of wildlife.

Hagood, Susan (Wildlife issues specialist), *State Wildlife Management: The Pervasive Influence of Hunters, Hunting, Culture and Money*, 1997

Many hunters talk about their mutuality of respect for wildlife. That's always sounded to me like phony baloney, else they would take on the big game hand-to-hand instead of with huge guns with scope sights...As for the argument that nature in the raw is cruel—of course it is! But we are supposed to be something more than they! Dickensian compassion rescued children from sweat shops. Lincolnian empathy rescued slaves from being 'things.' Civilization weeps while it awaits one more emancipation.

Harvey, Paul (Radio newscaster), from his syndicated column, November 1981

I was in a radio studio a little while ago, waiting to be interviewed. All morning, they had been having a phone-in on the subject of fox-hunting, and now I was listening to an interview with a wonderful man who had gone out from England to Bosnia, in an effort to raise the money to rebuild a bombed orphanage. Three times in that chat, the interviewer made the point that now they were talking about an issue that really mattered, after spending so much of the morning talking about fox-hunting. He clearly thought that the horrors of fox-hunting were not as important as the horrors of Bosnia. But what is the difference except in degree? The same state of mind, the same lack of respect for self and others, is behind both situations....Respect for all life, no matter what form it may take, will mean that the fox-hunter will cease to kill the fox and the Bosnian will cease to kill other Bosnians who don't share his culture, religion and ethnic inheritance.

Icke, David (Author), *Heal the World*, 1993

It is very strange, and very melancholy, that the paucity of human pleasures should persuade us ever to call hunting one of them.

Johnson, Samuel, 1909-1784 (English biographer and poet), quoted in *Birkbeck Hill's Johnsonian Miscellanies*

[Reported remark while admiring fish in an aquarium] Now I can look at you in peace; I don't eat you anymore.

Kafka, Franz, 1883-1924 (Visionary fiction writer)

Happy hunters do it in the name of recreation, holist hunters do it in the name of work, and holy hunters do it in the name of spirituality or religion. But despite these variations in language and emphasis, all three types of hunters include violence as an integral part of their ethical code, as long as it is restrained, renamed, or denied.

Kheel, Marti (Writer), in *Animals & Women*, 1995

When a man wantonly destroys one of the works of man, we call him a vandal. When he wantonly destroys one of the works of God, we call him a sportsman.

Krutch, Joseph Wood (American naturalist), 1893-1970, *The Great Chain of Life*, 1957

How anyone can profess to find animal life interesting and yet take delight in reducing the wonder of any animal to a bloody mass of fur and feathers is beyond my comprehension.

Ibid

Those who encourage fishing as a way to instill in their children a 'love of nature' are cheating them out of one of life's greatest pleasures: cultivating a true appreciation of the fragility of the planet and all of its various inhabitants.

Lewis, Nathan (Parent and ex-angler), letter, March 31, 1990

Throughout the country, special interests seeking to forestall the decline of hunting, the makers of arms and the state agencies that depend on hunters to justify their existence, are attempting to portray hunting as the solution to the decline of family values....Somehow, placing a three-foot long gun in the hands of a four-foot tall boy seems an odd solution to the crises of a violent society.

Lockwood, Randall, Ph.D. (Ethologist), 1989

Did you ever see a man and woman bow-hunter fire at several deer being fed in a yard, their arrows hitting the house and woodpile, barely missing humans? I did....Did you ever see a hunter cutting off the hindquarters of a wounded doe while she watched him? I did....Why did the Indian discard the bow and arrow 100 years ago for the rifle, only to have the white man take up the bow and arrow?...A treed bear looking like a pincushion, suffering excruciating pain with every arrow that entered his body—can you call this sport? Can the hunter be proud of such a cruel kill?...Why encourage our youth to participate in bow-hunting butchery? What is more nauseating than to see a full-grown man in a camouflage suit sneaking up to get a shot at a five-month old fawn? The cruelty of bow-hunting is completely indefensible, and when the book of life is closed on those who sanction it, they may pray for more merciful judgment than they are giving our wildlife, who have no voice of their own to plead their cause.

Marnich, J. R. (Former hunter), quoted in *Mankind?*, 1974

The Wisconsin Conservation Department, with their budget reaching toward half a hundred million dollars, does not need the blood-soaked dollars from the bow-hunting season. For every deer they kill quickly, at least five or six die lingering, agonizing, gruesome deaths.

Marty, Carl (Proprietor of a hotel resort at Three Lakes, Wisconsin), quoted in *Mankind?*, 1974

They were shooting pigeons. What an image of our condition, the loud report, the poor flopping bundles upon the ground, trying desperately, helplessly, vainly to rise again. How hardening to the heart it must be to do this thing: to change an innocent soaring being into a bundle of struggling rags and pain.

Murdoch, Iris (British novelist and philosopher), *The Black Prince*, 1973

The Church Assembly is of the opinion that the practices of

hare coursing, deer hunting and other hunting are cruel, unjustifiable and degrading and urges Christian people in the light of their Christian profession and responsibility to make plain their opposition to activities of this sort and their determination to do all in their power to secure their speedy abolition.

National Assembly of the Church of England, Report by the Board for Social Responsibility, 1970

Hunting...the least honourable form of war on the weak.

Paul, Richard, 1874-1939, *The Scourge of Christ*

We should find it hard to vindicate the destroying of anything that has life, merely out of sport. Yet in this principle children are bred, and one of the first pleasures we allow them is the licence of inflicting pain upon defenceless animals. Almost as soon as we are sensible what life is ourselves, we make it our sport to take it from others.

Pope, Alexander, 1688-1744 (English poet), *The Guardian*, May 1713

When will we reach the point that hunting, the pleasure of killing animals for sport, will be regarded as a mental aberration? We must reach the point that killing for sport will be felt as a disgrace to our civilization.

Schweitzer, Albert, Ph.D., M.D., 1875-1965 (Nobel Peace Prize-winning humanitarian), *The Teaching of Reverence for Life*

Custom will reconcile people to any atrocity; and fashion will drive them to acquire any custom.

Shaw, George Bernard, 1856-1950 (Nobel Prize-winning author), preface, "Killing for Sport"

I'm often astonished when I read about highly sensitive poets, preachers of morality, humanists and do-gooders of all kinds who found pleasure in hunting—chasing after some poor, weak hare or fox and teaching others to do likewise. I often read of people who say that when they retire they will go fishing. They say this with an understanding that from then on they won't do any damage to anybody. An epoch of charity and tranquillity will begin in their life. It never occurs to them for a moment that innocent beings will suffer and die from this innocent little sport.

Singer, Isaac Bashevis, 1904-1991 (Nobel Prize-winning author), foreword to *Vegetarianism, A Way of Life*, by Dudley Giehl

The use of the term 'harvest'—often found in the publications of the hunters' organizations—gives the lie to the claim that this slaughter is motivated by concern for the animals. The term indicates that the hunter thinks of deer or seals as if they were corn or coal, objects of interest only in so far as they serve human interests.

Singer, Peter, Ph.D. (Professor of Philosophy, Monash University, Australia), *Animal Liberation*, 1975

Animals give me more pleasure through the viewfinder of a camera than they ever did in the crosshairs of a gunsight. And after I've finished 'shooting,' my unharmed victims are still around for others to enjoy. I have developed a deep respect for animals. I consider them fellow living creatures with certain rights that should not be violated any more than those of humans.

Stewart, Jimmy, 1908-1997 (Actor),*The Readers Digest,* 1975

To be on friendly terms even with a sparrow is a keener satisfaction than the chase ever gave me....The ghastly memories of all the game I ever in my wild life slaughtered do not give me the pleasure which I have found in teaching a wild creature to forget its inheritance of fear of mankind and trust itself to my tenderness.

Stillman, W. J. (American journalist), *Plea for Wild Animals*, 1899

I implore every Field Archer, to make his own contribution to universal peace by bringing his portion of the world's violence and destruction of life to an end.

Stoughton, William L. (Retired army colonel), quoted in *Mankind?*, 1974

I have found repeatedly, of late years, that I cannot fish without falling a little in self-respect. I have tried it again and again. I have skill at it, and like many of my fellows, a certain instinct for it, which revives from time to time, but always when I have done [it] I feel it would have been better if I had not fished. I think that I do not mistake. It is a faint intimation, yet so are the first streaks of morning.

Thoreau, Henry D., 1817-1862 (American poet and philosopher), *Walden*

The squirrel that you kill in jest, dies in earnest.

Thoreau, Henry D., 1817-1862 (American poet and philosopher), *Familiar Letters*

Could not one spend some weeks or years in the solitude of this vast wilderness with other employments than these....For one that comes with a pencil to sketch, or sing, a thousand come with an axe or rifle. What a coarse and imperfect use hunters make of Nature!

Thoreau, Henry D., 1817-1862 (American poet and philosopher), *The Maine Woods*

I wanted to see what had become of my hunting instinct....After forty years of it, it is very pleasant to ride out and search for game. But when a hare jumped up, I merely wished him God-speed. The main thing is, one is ashamed.

Tolstoy, Leo Nikolayevich, 1828-1910 (Russian novelist), letter, 1884

Hunters' self-serving arguments and lies are becoming more preposterous as nonhunters awake from their long, albeit troubled, sleep. Sport hunting is immoral; it should be made illegal. Hunters are persecutors of nature who should be prosecuted. They wield a disruptive power out of all pro-portion to their numbers, and pandering to their interests — the special interests of a group that just wants to kill things — is mad. It's preposterous that every year less than 7 percent of the population turns the skies into shooting galleries and the woods and fields into abattoirs. It's time to stop actively supporting and passively allowing hunting, and time to stig-matize it. It's time to stop being conned and cowed by hunters, time to stop pampering and coddling them, time to get them off the government's duck-and-deer dole, time to stop thinking of wild animals as 'resources' and 'game,' and start thinking of them as sentient beings that deserve our wonder and respect, time to stop allowing hunting to be creditable by calling it 'sport' and 'recreation.' Hunters make wildlife *dead, dead, dead*. It's time to wake up to this indisputable fact.

Williams, Joy (Writer), "The Killing Game," *Esquire*, October 1990

souls like ourselves

11. TRAPPING, FUR FARMING AND FASHION

*T*he American Veterinary Medical Association considers the steel-jaw leghold trap to be inhumane.

American Veterinary Medical Association, position statement, *JAVMA*, Vol. 203, No. 3, August 1, 1993

Although arguments for killing wild and captive animals for their furs abound, particularly for so-called wildlife management practices, the sole purpose for peeling the furs from tormented animals—from those that are trapped, shot, poisoned and clubbed, to those confined in unnatural conditions on ranches is economic; the fur industry is a ruthless business feeding on human vanity.

Amory, Cleveland, 1917-1998 (Author and President, The Fund for Animals), 1988

The leghold trap is deceptively simple in appearance and the principle on which it works is also simple. The 'jaws' are opened by pressing on the spring, and the trap is set either on the trail of the animal, in its burrow or den, or close to a 'bait' or strong-smelling lure. The triggering device is the 'pan,' which, when the animal steps on it, releases the spring so that the jaws snap closed on his leg. From that moment on, the best the animal can hope for is to chew off his leg—the trappers call this 'wring-off'—so he can get away leaving just part of the leg behind. If he cannot do this—and indeed when he makes any movement of his paw between the jaws, the result is an immediate cutting, tearing and soring of flesh and even bone—the animal may remain in the trap for days on end, sometimes weeks, enduring every possible variety of fear, pain and suffering, until it finally dies either by exhaustion, starvation, cold, heat or the attacks of other animals, or is killed by the trapper.

Amory, Cleveland, 1917-1998 (Author and President, The Fund for Animals), *Mankind? Our Incredible War on Wildlife*, 1974

The wearing of any kind of skins — even the kind that are supposedly raised for fur, like mink or sable — is something I just don't believe in. Killing animals for vanity I think is a shame. I feel very guilty about having worn fur coats. As for the women who know about our vanishing wildlife and continue to buy fur coats — I wonder how *they'd* like to be skinned?...People are putting the whole real fur thing down and I thank God...thank God.

Blake, Amanda, 1927-1989 (Actress), interview

You must forgive me if I equate the two, but what the drug traffic is to the human race, the fur trade is to the animal kingdom. Happily we don't have to equate the two or choose between them. We can hate and fight both the drug racket and the fur industry. Workers in both fields will have to develop new skills.

Caras, Roger (President, American Society for the Prevention of Cruelty to Animals)

It is sometimes said, in defense of the use of the steel trap, that wildlife is cruel, and that the animals to whom the trap causes suffering, die a painful death anyway, by the teeth or claws of the predaceous species. But, great as the sufferings are of the animals that die a natural death, the sufferings occasioned by the common steel trap are incomparably greater. It is impossible for me to estimate the aggregate number of animals tortured by the common steel trap....I write this in 1946, and I recall the long Russian front, and other battlefields where millions of men were wounded, the bombing of German and British cities...and yet I think the annual sufferings of trapped animals in North America alone are greater than those caused by any war in Europe to mankind, over an equal period of time.

Conibear, Frank (Famous trapper from British Columbia), *Testimony of a Trapper*, 1946

The foot is lacerated, swollen and covered with blood. The stump of the leg above the trap is swollen four times its natural size, and frozen. The shoulder, too, is all swollen. When we skin it, we will find that all that area will be a mass of blood-colored, sickly gelatin-like substance, indicating the terrible suffering it has gone through before death released it.

Ibid

A woman gains status when she refuses to see anything killed to be put on her back. Then she's truly beautiful!

Day, Doris (Actress and founder, Doris Day Animal League), newspaper interview

My respect for an animal's right to live doesn't let me approve of the killing of animals for coats. If a woman can help an animal or a child, that's the most important thing.

Dickinson, Angie (Actress), interview

In this world each creature has been apportioned one skin. Who can argue with that kind of economy?...We have no need, no excuse for robbing beautiful creatures of their skins, no matter how luxuriant they may be. Each being has need of its own outside.

Gist, Reverend Richard (Minister and writer), 1994

I cannot stand the idea that wild animals can be killed to satisfy fashion.

Grace of Monoco, Princess, 1929-1982

No one really needs a mink coat in this world...except minks.

Jackson, Glenda (Actress), newspaper interview

When you buy fur, you really strike out.

La Russa, Tony (Oakland A's [baseball] manager), 1990

An English trapper [later known as Grey Owl] came to America long ago and fell in love with the country and with a lovely Iroquois woman named Anahareo. One day he found a mother beaver in one of his traps and nearby two tiny beaver kits. At his wife's urging, he took the two tiny beaver babies home with him. During the course of raising them he realized he would never hunt animals again. At the time of this decision he wrote: 'Their almost childlike intimacies and murmurings of affection, their rollicking good fellowship not only with each other but ourselves, their keen awareness, their air of knowing what it was all about. They seemed like little folk from some other planet, whose language we could not quite understand. To kill such creatures seemed monstrous. I would do no more of it.'

Laland, Stephanie (Author), *Peaceful Kingdom*, 1997

I feel very sad for women who continue to purchase real fur coats. They are lacking in a woman's most important requisites, heart and sensitivity.

Meadows, Jayne (Actress), interview

The killing of an animal for the sake of appearance of luxury doesn't achieve anything.

Moore, Mary Tyler (Actress), interview

It's unbelievable the amount of non-target species that are taken by leg-hold traps and the torture that follows when they are in the trap. Anything that comes by and steps in the trap with a foot small enough to fit between the jaws is going to become a victim.

Randall, Dick (Former professional trapper), 1994

[Commentary on Canada's baby seal hunt] It's a hell of a thing. It's a particularly hellish thing when you've got what amounts to an open-air slaughterhouse. What you've got to do is stop telling people to write letters to Canada and Norway. Tell them instead to start a worldwide campaign against the wearing of furs.

Rowsell, Dr. Harry (Veterinary Pathologist), Seals and Sealing Committee, Canadian Ministry of Fisheries, 1973

There's that word again! [harvest] We persist in using the euphemism wherever the slaughtering of attractive animals is being talked about. Dammit, we kill them. We slaughter them, just like we slaughter cattle. We catch them in steel traps or blow them down with shotguns. We rip off their hides and wear their furs or hang their heads on den walls.

We *kill them*, we don't *harvest them*!! Someday we'll all grow up and face that reality.

Waller, Robert James (Author, *The Bridges of Madison County*),
The Des Moines Register, April 27, 1988

I love all animals. I haven't bought a fur since 1956.

West, Mae, 1893-1980 (Actress/Entertainer)

souls like ourselves

o release our wild animals from the bondage of the arms man-
ufacturers and the gun and ammo magazines many things
must be done. State laws against cruelty to animals must be
applied to wild animals—as they were originally intended to
do—and they must be upheld by the courts. Fish and Game
departments must be reconstituted, so that the nonhunter
may be not only represented, but represented in the proportion that his numbers warrant. State conservation and nat-
ural-resources commissions too must be totally reorganized.
They have no business in the promotion of this billion-dollar
butchery. The animals themselves must be legally realigned.
The animals do not 'belong' to your individual state. Then
too, the Federal Government's U.S. Fish and Wildlife
'Service' must be, in reality, a service. It has taught the whole
world 'game management;' now it must get out of the 'game'
and unteach the 'management.' And, finally, if the National
Rifle Association insists to the very end that the slaughter of
animals is basic to its cause concerning the right to bear arms,
then that cause, or the organization, or both, must go.

Amory, Cleveland, 1917-1998 (Author and President, The Fund
for Animals), *Mankind? Our Incredible War on Wildlife*, 1974

Perhaps the time has come to formulate a moral code which
would govern our relations with the great creatures of the sea
as well as those on dry land. That this will come to pass is our
dearest wish....If civilization is going to invade the waters of
the earth, then let it be first of all to carry a message of
respect—respect for all life.

Cousteau, Jacques-Yves, 1910-1997 (French oceanographer),
The Whale: Mighty Monarch of the Sea

Divers who have swum with them frequently report feeling as if the whales were protecting and taking care of them. In one amazing incident off Hawaii in March, 1976, a female whale asked for help. The 'White Bird' was carrying divers when a giant humpback whale knocked her head on the boat three or four times, diver Roy Nickerson reported. After each knock, she would withdraw, and raise herself to look up at those on deck. He donned his wetsuit and went down to investigate. He found she had aborted, and her baby calf was stillborn, but not free of her body. Other divers then went down, lassoed the dead calf, and pulled it clear. It was a sad incident, but illustrative of the co-operation that could exist between our species, if we wanted it.

Cox, Peter (British author), *The New Why You Don't Need Meat,* 1992

They [gorillas] are brave and loyal. They help each other. They rival elephants as parents and whales for gentleness. They play and have humour and they harm nothing. They are what we should be. I don't know if we'll ever get there.

Derby, Pat (Former animal trainer), *The Lady and her Tiger,* 1976

Wild animals are not meant to be owned, any more than human beings are. Nobody has the right to pass a cougar or a gorilla on from hand to hand.

Ibid

It is not enough to feel disgusted. Do not say how scandalous it all is and shed a furtive tear: act individually by boycotting all institutions that exploit fauna. Above all, do not buy any more animals, not one single animal more; don't go to the zoo, don't go to the circus.

Domlaim, Jean-Yves, *The Animal Connection: The Confessions of an Ex-Wild Animal Trafficker*

I feel more comfortable with gorillas than people. I can anticipate what a gorilla's going to do, and they're purely motivated.

Fossey, Dian, 1940-1985 (American zoologist), interview, 1980

We know quite enough facts now; where we are still miserably retarded is in our emotional and aesthetic relationship to wildlife. Nature is a sort of art sans art; and the right human attitude to it ought to be, unashamedly, poetic rather than scientific.

Fowles, John (British novelist), 1971

The world's largest brains are found in cetacean and not human skulls, and the toothed whales or dolphins have brains that are roughly comparable in size and complexity to our own....It is counterintuitive to deny that they think consciously about some of their activities as it would be to advance such an absurd claim about the Great Apes.

Griffin, Donald R. (Professor of Zoology, Cornell University, Harvard University and the Rockefeller University), *Animal Minds*, 1992

What profit do we have if we gain the whole world and lose or forfeit our own souls? The human race may survive without the chimpanzees, orangutans, and other wild creatures who share the planet. But we will have attenuated the conditions that are necessary for our own 'ensoulment.' We will have traded a nurturing family for a dys-spirited one. The ecology of mind will not be as vivifying and luxuriant. And when we look into the mirror there will be less and less to love.

Kowalski, Gary (Unitarian Universalist minister), *The Souls of Animals*, 1991

Because mother dolphins nurse their young for so long—eighteen months or about as long as human mothers nurse—the mother-child bond is very strong. Many times a dolphin will not desert another dolphin who is in trouble even if it costs them their own life. When infant dolphins are trapped in tuna nets, their mothers will try desperately to join them. Then the mothers will cuddle close to their babies and sing to them as they both drown. The tuna industry's official acknowledgment of this remarkable phenomenon is that most of the dolphins killed are mothers and infants.

Laland, Stephanie (Author), *Peaceful Kingdom*, 1997

How many compassionate epicures would dine on lobsters knowing that in the wild they live for as long as 100 years in social units, feeding and altruistically caring for injured members of their society? How delectable would be the dining if people knew that the lobsters who are boiled alive have intricate nervous systems and thrash about the boiling water for over a minute before they finally die?

McFarland, Cole (Writer and editor), 1991

Lobsters are fascinating. They have a long childhood and an awkward adolescence. They use complicated signals to explore and establish social relationships with others....Like us, lobsters are vertebrates who feel pain; when they are tossed into scalding water, their claws scrape the sides of the pot as they struggle to get out.

Newkirk, Ingrid (National Director, People for the Ethical Treatment of Animals), *Save the Animals!*, 1990

I would not be comfortable appearing in a country where they have permitted the destruction of such beautiful and intelligent mammals.

Newton-John, Olivia (Singer), newspaper interview after her 1978 cancellation of a tour to Japan because of their dolphin kill

If the world [human] population continues to expand at its present rate, there is absolutely no hope whatsoever that wildlife is going to survive.

Philip, Prince (Duke of Edinburgh), radio interview, April 20, 1986

I worked for the Department of Interior Fish and Wildlife Service for ten years as an animal damage control agent. I used poisons, aerial hunting, trapping, denning, all kinds of things to destroy what they call 'predatory wildlife.' We had a war on the species going—any coyote was bad. Anytime you collected a set of ears—killed a coyote, poisoned a coyote—that was good, regardless of whether it was doing any damage or not. I have a lot of memories...things that I did that were not necessary...which the government said was just right on...and that's one of the things I have so many problems with, is that a person can get involved in this and believe they are doing the right thing. They're saving the livestock industry. That's bull manure! All you're doing is killing wildlife and its been going on since 1915 with the taxpayer's money and it's never solved any problems....There are alternatives to killing wildlife. Other ways to protect livestock. But you can shoot a hole in a coyote and see the blood and I think that makes people feel better sometimes.

Randall, Dick (Former professional trapper), 1994

13. ENTERTAINMENT, EXHIBITION AND WORK ANIMALS

Everybody in the greyhound business without exception—there is not the first one that doesn't—take their dogs and kill them. I've had several people tell me, "You know for the price of a twenty two bullet, I can take care of all of them for you. You just bring them to me and I'll shoot them and dump them in a hole." The case they had in Ocala [Florida] just recently [196 greyhounds found in cages dying of starvation in addition to buried remains of other greyhounds]...this happens all the time. You only hear about a small number of the cases where these dogs are improperly taken care of.

Anonymous former greyhound breeder turned humane society undercover investigator, "Greyhounds: running for their lives," National Geographic Explorer: The Canine Connection, airing on TBS, Spring 1994

The minute they [racing greyhounds] can't cut it, they are automatically done away with in the most horrendous ways....They are so gentle...so loving...it upsets me terribly....The only way they [the greyhound industry] are going to change is to do away completely with greyhound racing, so I really feel that it must, sooner or later, be outlawed totally.

Arthur, Bea (Actress), interview, 1994

Greyhounds are bred for mass destruction; 70 percent are killed before they even reach the racetrack. If collies or golden retrievers were being slaughtered, people would be up in arms.

Baker, Bob (Humane investigator), interview, 1991

[Of the claim that rodeo is Americana] So was slavery, cannibalism in the Donner Pass, the Bad Day at Black Rock, prohibition, the slaughter of the American Indian and the wasting of their priceless culture, the slaughter of the bison and the whale, lynching blacks, the Ku Klux Klan, Father Coughlin, Joe McCarthy and the Vigilantes...all Americana. Is that enough excuse for a cultural artifact to persist?

Caras, Roger (President, American Society for the Prevention of Cruelty to Animals)

Kindness and compassion towards all living things is a mark of a civilized society. Conversely, cruelty, whether it is directed against human beings or against animals, is not the exclusive province of any one culture or community of people....Racism, economic deprival, dog-fighting and cockfighting, bullfighting and rodeos are cut from the same fabric: violence....Only when we have become non-violent towards all life will we have learned to live well ourselves.

Chavez, Cesar, 1927-1993 (Farm labor leader awarded U.S. Medal of Freedom), letter, December 1990

It is our contention that zoos in fact do very little for conservation and that they are merely the providers of an outdated and cruel method of entertainment...We hope you will help us in our fight to make zoos take responsibility for the industry they have created and the appalling suffering they cause to millions of animals around the world.

Dickson, Andrew (Chief Executive, World Society for the Protection of Animals), 1994

Even the best of zoos cannot justify their existence if they do not sufficiently inform and even shock the public into compassionate concern and political action. I know of no zoo that exhibits crippled but otherwise healthy animals that have been maimed by trappers and hunters.

Fox, Michael W., D.Sc., Ph.D., B.Vet.Med. (Ethologist), *Inhumane Society*, 1990

We should need no zoos and we are misguided if we do not work toward this end, however far into the future it might be. Zoos are not so much a necessary evil as they are a tragic mirror of an evil for which we may yet atone.

Ibid

There can be no communion with our animal kin when they are held captive, no matter what the justifications may be for their 'protective custody.' The zoo is a trick mirror that can delude us into believing that we love and respect animals and are helping to preserve them. And like the animal circus, the zoo can have a pernicious influence on children's attitudes toward wild creatures.

Ibid

As we demean animals in making them perform unnatural acts, so we demean ourselves. The training, which is often brutal, and the socialization to the trainer, which is unnatural, in the course of subordinating performing animals to the will of the trainer is like a ritual enactment of humanity's control over the forces of nature....Even if the trainer or animal handler loves the animals, as soon as they begin to perform, what is manifested is not love but domination. Domination — the need to have power and control over other beings — comes not from love but from fear. Most fundamentally, performing animals, therefore, are an expression not of human love and understanding but of fear, ignorance, and the desire for power and control.

Ibid

Professionally managed captive-breeding programs do not exist at most zoos. Indeed, the majority of zoos only breed animals because managers fail to control breeding, or to provide income, or so there will be baby animals born each year....Frequently, those indiscriminately bred surplus zoo animals end up in horrendous situations. They may change hands at an exotic-animal auction where they endure transport to and from the auction site in cages that can cause injuries. They are then sold to the highest bidder with no regard to the quality of care they will receive....They may be sold to game ranches where they are hunted as trophies. They may end up in roadside zoos, where they are neglected or abused and maintained in wretched conditions. They also may end up with private individuals who have no experience in keeping exotic animals. Frequently these animals die or go from one miserable situation to another; from circuses to performing animal acts to shopping-center photo exhibits.

Grandy, John, Ph.D. (Wildlife biologist), 1989

[Discarded rodeo animals were] so extensively bruised that the only areas in which the skin was attached [to the flesh] was the head, neck, leg and belly. I have seen animals with six to eight ribs broken from the spine and, at times, puncturing the lungs. I have seen as much as two to three gallons of free blood accumulated under the detached skin.

Haber, D. C., D.V.M. (Veterinarian and federal meat inspector), interview, 1979

It took me nearly 60 years to outgrow the circus. I made the break last year with help from a woman named Florence Lambert [The Elephant Alliance]. She asked that I try to see the elephants and other circus animals as she sees them: exploited and abused creatures....Indeed, once you start viewing circus animals as exploited beings, it is difficult to view them as anything else. We're talking about tigers in cramped cages, horses and zebras put through frenzied and uninteresting performances, elephants made to kick up their hind legs and beg like cocker spaniels....Subsequent research and interviews with animal welfare experts convinced me that Lambert was right about the exploitation and abuse of circus animals....I won't try to talk you out of seeing the circus...but try seeing the animals as Lambert does. You may find that you, too, have outgrown the Brothers Ringling.

Hennessy, Tom (Newspaper columnist), July 17, 1996

I believe that the inevitable circumstances of whales and dolphins in captivity are among the most visible forms of cruelty that any of us see. There is simply no way...to maintain these magnificent animals in captivity without accepting the most incredible barbarism. These are animals who may naturally swim 50 to 100 miles per day; dive to incredible depths; and live in close knit family societies for their entire lives. Captivity destroys their families and robs them of every aspect of their natural environment...and of life. We need...to ensure that everyone understands that an orca breaching in a concrete tank or a dolphin eating dead fish in an aquarium are not symbols of beauty and fun, but symbols of cruelty.

Irwin, Paul G. (President, The Humane Society of the United States), speech, 1995

To what degree does education require keeping wild animals in captivity? Couldn't most of the educational benefits of zoos be obtained by presenting films, slides, lectures and so forth? Indeed, couldn't most of the important educational objectives better be achieved by exhibiting empty cages with explanations of why they are empty?...Zoos teach us a false sense of our place in the natural order. The means of confinement mark a difference between humans and animals. They are there at our pleasure, to be used for our purposes. Morality and perhaps our very survival require that we learn to live as one species among many rather than as one species over many. To do this, we must forget what we learn at zoos. Because what zoos teach us is false and dangerous, both humans and animals will be better off when they are abolished.

Jamieson, Dale (Professor of Philosophy, University of Colorado), *In Defense of Animals*, Peter Singer, ed., 1985

The shackled tormented life of a circus elephant is demeaning, not only to the animals, but to humankind as well. Too long have we buried our heads in the sand of ignorance....Only a sensitive and enlightened public will stop the exploitation of circus elephants and other animals.

Lambert, Florence L. (Director, The Elephant Alliance), 1993

Circus elephants are totally, neurotically insane. [They] have no life. Every natural behavior they have is thwarted.

Landres, Lisa (Former elephant keeper at San Diego [California] Zoo), 1995

I hesitate to call it a sport. Rodeo is a constant and persistent inhumane treatment of animals....The nature of the competition in a rodeo depends on the performance of the animal, and the only way to get the horses and calves to perform the way they do is to use cruel and tormenting methods.

Larson, Peggy, D.V.M. (Former rodeo rider and veterinarian who treats rodeo animals), interview, 1998

souls like ourselves

I don't think you should hurt or kill animals just to entertain an audience. Animals should have some rights. But there are a lot of directors...who will injure animals to further a plot. I will have none of it.

Mason, James, 1909-1984 (Actor), quote in late 1980, explaining why he refused to play opposite Sophia Loren in a film containing a cock-fighting sequence

It is the sadness of zoos which haunts me. The purposeless existence of the animals....This is not conservation—and surely it is not education. No, this is 'entertainment.' Not comedy, however, but tragedy.

McKenna, Virginia (Film actress and founder, Born Free Foundation), *Beyond the Bars: The Zoo Dilemma*, 1988

Keeping elephants in captivity is an outrage.

Mugford, Roger, Ph.D. (Animal psychologist), quoted by Florence Lambert, 1993

The cruel wild beast is not behind the bars of the cage. He stands in front of it.

Munthe, Dr. Axel, 1857-1949 (Swedish physician and writer)

The [greyhound racing] industry claims that their problems are based upon public relations difficulties. What they really have is a reality problem....Most greyhounds don't live to be retirement age which is five years. The majority are put to death at two, three and four years of age.

Netboy, Susan (Founder, Greyhound Protection League), interview, 1991

Wielding a slender sword the matador moved forward to finish off the stricken bull. His first attempt left a deep wound in the side of the animal. The bull made a loud howling noise as the blade pierced its lungs....[The matador] attempted to stay calm, enacting a series of grotesque poses to show the discipline of his so called art; but after several more failed attempts, the thrusts of his sword became more and more desperate....The crowd grew restless. The bull was exhausted and recoiled in pain. Unable to charge, it stared in confusion at the red cape. The eighth stab must have found the bull's heart and it slowly collapsed, choking on blood....The spectators at the small arena in St. Gilles [France], whom I could only assume were otherwise normal people, showed no concern or pity for the animal.

Pearce, Jonathan (Editor, *Animals International*), 1998

As someone who frequented dog tracks for the last 20 years, I never dreamed I would be writing this, but it is time that states stop licensing greyhound racing until the industry cleans up its act.

Rand, Jonathan (Journalist), 1989

The captive display of marine mammals provides poor or even false education. Certain species never adjust to confinement, contrary to the claims of the captive display industry. It is extremely difficult to justify keeping marine mammals, particularly the wholly aquatic cetacean species, in sterile tanks that do not even remotely resemble their natural habitat. The only conclusion, therefore, is that wild marine mammals belong in only one place: the ocean.

Rose, Naomi A., Ph.D. (Marine mammal scientist), 1996

Even after living in cages, they [greyhounds] love people....I've never seen a breed like them.

Schnepf, Dale, D.V.M. (Veterinarian and greyhound rescuer), interview, September 23, 1991

The exhibiting of trained animals I abhor. What an amount of suffering and cruel punishment the poor creatures have to endure in order to give a few moments of pleasure to men devoid of all thought and feeling.

Schweitzer, Albert, Ph.D., M.D., 1875-1965 (Nobel Peace Prize-winning humanitarian), *Memoirs of Childhood and Youth*, 1949

It is a disgrace to our time that animal fights are still being staged everywhere, including bull fights and cock fights and other cruel diversions.

Schweitzer, Albert, Ph.D., M.D., 1875-1965 (Nobel Peace Prize-winning humanitarian), *The Animal World of Albert Schweitzer*, 1950

For an elephant, a quality of life is S-P-A-C-E, and no elephant can be given adequate space in captivity. Most circus and zoo elephants end up tragic psychotics. Wouldn't we, were we subjected to the same abuse?

Sheldrick, Daphne, M.B.E. (Wildlife rehabilitator in Nairobi, Kenya), letter, 1997

It is unusual to see tears running from eyes of wild elephants, although it is common in captive specimens...

Sikes, Dr. Sylvia K., *The Natural History of the African Elephant*, 1971

In ten years, people will look back at what we did with exotic animals in circuses with astonishment and revulsion.

Suzuki, David T., Ph.D. (Professor of Zoology, University of British Columbia), letter, 1997

The elephant has been reduced to a bowdlerized Dumbo-Jumbo, a performing slave in a designer cage, with its tusks sawn off and a ring through a piece of flesh sensitive enough to read Braille.

Williams, Heathcote (Author), *Sacred Elephant*, 1989

souls like ourselves

14. SOCIAL
JUSTICE AND
CHANGE

ost of us would be horrified if a neighbor did to her companion animal what is routinely—and in most cases, legally—inflicted on literally millions of animals daily, not only in laboratories and in the wild, but in factory farms, transport and slaughterhouses. Most of us view ourselves as reasonably humane. While we of course act out of self-interest as well, a good deal of our politics comes from an altruistic desire for a more just and humane society; our natural kindness is repelled by the plethora of horrors we see in the world, directly or through the media....We have been blinded by speciesism to the suffering of non-human animals, just as racism, sexism, etc., prevent 'non-target' dominant groups from seeing and feeling the agonized realities of subjugated human classes.

Boyd, Billy Ray (Author), *The New Abolitionists*

My pain in the head remains more vivid to me than your pain in the head, but if I adjust for this I have to perceive that your hitting me and my hitting you are acts in exactly the same class; I can't deplore the one without deploring the other; I have weighed them in a balance as accurate as I can make it, found them to be equally bad, and have thereby set irreversibly out towards social justice....To my mind, therefore, there was both a logical and a psychological inevitability in basing the claim for other animals' rights on social justice.

Brophy, Brigid, 1929-1995 (British novelist), *Animals' Rights: A Symposium*

See every difficulty as a challenge, a stepping stone, and

never be defeated by anything or anyone.

Caddy, Eileen, *The Dawn of Change*, 1979

The individual is capable of both great compassion and great indifference. He has it within his means to nourish the former and outgrow the latter....Nothing is more powerful than an individual acting out of his conscience, thus helping to bring the collective conscience to life.

Cousins, Norman (Author and former editor, *Saturday Review*), *Human Options*, 1988

Animals, whom we have made our slaves, we do not like to consider our equal.

Darwin, Charles, 1809-1882 (English naturalist), *Letters*

There is no force so powerful as an idea whose time has come.

Dirksen, Everett, 1896-1969 (U.S. politician), speech on civil rights bill, U.S. Senate, 1964

Just as feminists were charged with man-hating when we began to channel our energies and our theorizing to women's needs and experiences, animal activists now stand accused of people-hating. Such charges reveal anxiety about the moral content of the activism as well as ignorance about the underlying and interconnected roots of oppression.

Donovan, Josephine (Professor of English, University of Maine) and **Carol J. Adams** (Writer), introduction to *Animals & Women*, 1995

The realization that other animals share an inner world as reasonable and as sensible as ours, brings us to the precipice of a great and thrilling horizon. Humanity may be on the brink of granting to the jungle a blanket manumission, in the same way that European Whites finally became morally obligated to grant manumission to Black slaves....A growing number of people are realizing that the special spark of life we recognize burning in human beings may actually be burning just as brightly in all species.

Downs, Hugh (Emmy Award-winning journalist), news commentary, May 29, 1994

Women should be protected from anyone's exercise of unrighteous power...but then, so should every other living creature.

Eliot, George, 1819-1880 (English novelist), from a letter

Human liberation will begin when we understand that our evolution and fulfillment are contingent on the recognition of animal rights and on a compassionate and responsible stewardship of nature.

Fox, Michael W., D.Sc., Ph.D., B.Vet.Med. (Ethologist), *Returning to Eden*, 1979

As we enter the 21st century, we may receive unexpected repayments by taking today what some of you may consider heretical steps. *Or should we say revolutionary? like overturning old customs—such as animal slavery?*...Please let us not forget our relationship with all that lives. Remember the meaning of ecology: *we live in the house of life and all the rooms connect.*

Free, Ann Cottrell (Author and journalist), address, 1992

The awful wrongs and sufferings forced upon the innocent, helpless, faithful animal race, form the blackest chapter in the whole world's history.

Freeman, Edward Augustus, 1823-1892, *History of Europe*

Every civilizing step in history has been ridiculed as 'sentimental,' 'impractical,' 'womanish,' etc., by those whose fun, profit or convenience was at stake.

Gilbert, Joan (Author), letter in *American Horseman*

Why do I care so much? Why, in order to change attitudes and actions in the [research] labs, do I subject myself repeatedly to the personal nightmare of visiting these places...? The answer is simple....It is time to repay something of the debt I owe the chimpanzees.

Goodall, Jane, Ph.D. (Ethologist), quoted in *Animals & Women*, 1995

Ever occur to you why some of us can be this much concerned with animals' suffering? Because government is not. Why not? Animals don't vote.

Harvey, Paul (Radio newscaster), from his syndicated column,
January 1981

To help heal the Earth, you need only pause for a moment, look deep into yourself, and ask, "What's the right thing to do?" And then do it.

Hayes, Denis (American environmentalist and National Coordinator of the first Earth Day), speech on the Mall, Washington D.C., Earth Day 1990

Far more crucial than what we know or do not know is what we do not want to know.

Hofer, Eric, *The Passionate State of Mind*, 1954

Real progress is progress in charity, all other advances being secondary thereto.

Huxley, Aldous, 1894-1963 (English novelist), *Ends and Means*, 1937

Our treatment of animals will someday be considered barbarous. There cannot be perfect civilization until man realizes that the rights of every living creature are as sacred as his own.

Jordan, Dr. David Starr, 1851-1931 (Naturalist and educator), *The Days of Man*, 1922

We must combine the toughness of the serpent and softness of the dove, a tough mind and a tender heart.

King, Martin Luther, Jr., Ph.D., 1929-1968 (Nobel Peace Prize-winning civil rights leader), *Strength to Love*, 1963

To transform the world we must begin with ourselves.

Krishnamurti, Jiddu, 1895-1986 (Indian philosopher and spiritual leader)

What we need is progressive disengagement from our inhumanity to animals. The urgent and essential task is to invite, encourage, support and welcome those who want to take some steps along the road to a more peaceful world with the non-human creation.

Linzey, Reverend Dr. Andrew, Center for the Study of
Theology, University of Essex, U.K., *Christianity and the Rights of
Animals*, 1987

Never doubt that a small group of committed citizens can
change the world; indeed, it's the only thing that ever has.

Mead, Margaret, Ph.D., 1901-1978 (American anthropologist)

For the first time in civilized history, people who were inter-
ested in animals because they wanted to understand them,
rather than just to eat or yoke or shoot or stuff them, have been
able to advance that understanding by scientific means, and to
convey some of it to the inquisitive public....Town-dwellers are
beginning to notice the biosphere.

Midgley, Mary (Philosopher), *Animals and Why They Matter*, 1983

All great movements experience three stages: Ridicule.
Discussion. Adoption.

Mill, John Stuart, 1806-1873 (British philosopher)

Concerning all acts of initiative...there is one elementary truth,
the ignorance of which kills countless ideas and splendid
plans: that the moment one definitely commits oneself, then
providence moves too.

Murray, W. H., *The Scottish Himalayan Expedition*, 1951

People often ask me why I spend so much time protecting
the welfare of animals. They refer to my active support of
legislation to outlaw barbarism in packing plants...my
protesting liquidation of the famous White House
squirrels...urging a halt to the oil drilling and gas prospecting
taking place all over our national wildlife and waterfowl
refuges....I have several answers. The first is that Dr. Albert
Schweitzer...often said that one of the real symbols of a truly
civilized person is whether or not he is kind to
animals....Also I cite one of my favorite quotations from the
Bible: 'Verily I say unto you, inasmuch as ye have done it
unto one of the least of these my brethren, ye have done it
unto me.'....I have always believed that cruelty to beasts is a
black mark in heaven...particularly cruelty which is wanton

and totally unnecessary. I realize that animals, whether of the field or of the forest, do not vote. They do not make campaign contributions to enrich the coffers of politicians running for office. But I will be their friend. I imagine that he who spoke the Sermon on the Mount would want it that way too.

Neuberger, Senator Richard L., 1912-1960, Congressional address

We can disagree heartily as to what will bring about animal liberation the soonest, but all of us are guessing, so let's not try to undermine each other and be accusatory of each other's motives. We are, after all, walking along the same road, changing our behaviors as we go, stalling periodically, but trying to find the strength to do what we believe is right.

Newkirk, Ingrid (National Director, People for the Ethical Treatment of Animals), January 1992

We may have discovered the existence of radio sources several million light years away with an immensely clever piece of equipment, but we continue to treat each other and all other living things on our planet in a way which is only a bare improvement on primitive man....I want to suggest that scientific and technological progress is not only valueless, it is actively harmful, unless it is modified or directed by a social and humanitarian outlook.

Philip, Prince (Duke of Edinburgh), *Men, Machines and Sacred Cows*, 1984

That is the image of philosophy I would leave with you, not 'too cerebral' but *disciplined passion*. Of the discipline enough has been seen. As for the passion: there are times, and these not infrequent, when tears come to my eyes when I see, or read, or hear of the wretched plight of animals in the hands of humans. Their pain, their suffering, their loneliness, their innocence, their death. Anger. Rage. Pity. Sorrow. Disgust. The whole creation groans under the weight of the evil we humans visit upon these mute, powerless creatures. It *is* our hearts, not just our heads, that call for an end to it all, that demand of us that we overcome, for them, the habits and forces behind their systematic oppression. All great movements, it is written, go through three stages: ridicule, discussion, adoption. It is the realization of this third stage, adoption, that requires both our passion and our discipline, our hearts and our heads. The fate of the animals is in our hands. God grant we are equal to the task.

Regan, Dr. Tom (Professor of Philosophy, North Carolina State University), *In Defense of Animals*, Peter Singer, ed., 1985

There is no right to life in any society on Earth today, nor has there been at any former time. We raise animals for slaughter; destroy forests; pollute rivers and lakes until no fish can live there; hunt deer and elk for sport, leopards for their pelts, and whales for dog food; entwine dolphins, gasping and writhing, in great tuna nets; and club seal pups to death for 'population management.' All these beasts and vegetables are as alive as we. What is protected in many human societies is not life, but human life.

Sagan, Dr. Carl, 1934-1996 (U.S. astronomer), *The Dragons of Eden*, 1977

Man can no longer live for himself alone. We must realize that all life is valuable and that we are united to all life. From this knowledge comes our spiritual relationship with the universe.

Schweitzer, Albert, Ph.D., M.D., 1875-1965 (Nobel Peace Prize-winning humanitarian), *Christian Century*, Vol. 51, 1934

There will be no justice as long as man will stand with a knife or with a gun and destroy those who are weaker than he is.

Singer, Isaac Bashevis, 1904-1991 (Nobel Prize-winning author), foreword to *Vegetarianism, A Way of Life* by Dudley Giehl, 1979

This book [*Animal Liberation*] is about the tyranny of human over non-human animals. This tyranny has caused and today is still causing an amount of pain and suffering that can only be compared with that which resulted from the centuries of tyranny by white humans over black humans. The struggle against this tyranny is a struggle as important as any of the moral and social issues that have been fought over in recent years.

Singer, Peter, Ph.D. (Professor of Philosophy, Monash University), *Animal Liberation*, 1975

Human beings have the power to continue to oppress other species forever, or until we make this planet unsuitable for living beings. Will our tyranny continue, proving that we really are the selfish tyrants that the most cynical of poets and philosophers have always said we are? Or will we rise to the challenge and prove our capacity for genuine altruism by ending our ruthless exploitation of the species in our power, not because we are forced to do so by rebels or terrorists, but because we recognize that our position is morally indefensible?...The way in which we answer this question depends on the way in which each one of us, individually, answers it.

Ibid

The realization that the animals we enslave, the animals we turn into things, the animals who slave for us that we might eat some luxury from their bodies, are *alive*, are as possessive of their lives as you or I, this realization would throw a wrench into the system. If this realization were reached, people would have to change an aspect of their lifestyle. And this is why many people resist thinking about it, resist questioning the system, and fail to know the obvious. Which greatly pleases the slave-*owners*, those who directly profit from the lives of animals and from our passive and active acceptance of slavery and oppression. For if individuals did question it, and refused to participate any longer, the system would collapse.

Spiegel, Marjorie (Author), *The Dreaded Comparison: Human and Animal Slavery*, 1977

Basically the strategy in all struggles for freedom is similar. Generally, the other side has all the power, and the oppressed have only justice and the capacity to mobilize people on their side. To succeed, we need much expertise and credibility, and must carefully work out partial, short-term goals to reach people and effect the change we desire....Through meticulous preparation, a small group can release an enormous amount of energy.

Spira, Henry, 1927-1998 (Social activist), "Fighting for Animal Rights" in *Ethics and Animals*, 1983

It's like this guy from the *New York Times* asked me what I'd like my epitaph to be. I said, 'He pushed the peanut forward.' I try to move things on a little.

Spira, Henry, 1927-1998 (Social activist), *Ethics into Action: Henry Spira and the Animal Rights Movement*, Peter Singer, 1998, when asked how he would like to be remembered

All progress has resulted from people who took unpopular positions.

Stevenson, Adlai E., 1900-1965 (U.S. political leader), Princeton University speech, 1954

It's a matter of taking the side of the weak against the strong, something the best people have always done.

Stowe, Harriet Beecher, 1811-1896 (American writer and philanthropist), *The Minister's Wooing*

Loyalty to a petrified opinion never yet broke a chain or freed a human soul.

Twain, Mark, 1835-1910 (American humorist and writer)

All progressive legislation has always had its genesis in the mind of one person. In the long run it is the cumulative effect that matters. One can do much. And one and one and one can move mountains.

Ward-Harris, Joan (Author), *Creature Comforts*

As more humans awake to the deeper identity of other sentient beings, the seeds of evolution are created—seeds that will ultimately foster not only harmony between humans and other animals, but also between humans and other humans....The evolution of our species will mirror that of its individual members. As with other significant changes in social attitudes throughout history, the opposition will be formidable; the process will be cumbersome, costly, and frustrating; the means to achieving change will be varied; and

souls like ourselves

the road will be trying and sometimes discouraging. But, the result will be glorious.

Wiebers, David O., M.D. (Professor of Neurology, Mayo Clinic), speech, 1992

Working with others, I have committed my life in the endeavor...to alter the course of this world's cruelty to animals. It does not negate my passions for other causes. This just happens to be mine. I did not intellectually select it. It found me.

Wyler, Gretchen (Actress and President, The Ark Trust), speech, 1980

If we do not learn how to deflect the course of our violent, acquisitive society, we shall destroy not only our surroundings but ourselves. Merely to 'drop out' is a negative gesture. We must be prepared to contribute towards a better pattern—a civilized alternative.

Wynne-Tyson, Jon (English author and publisher), *The Civilised Alternative*, 1972

Acknowledgments

We wish to recognize and express our gratitude to Jon Wynne-Tyson, whose earlier work of quotations, *The Extended Circle, An Anthology of Humane Thought*, inspired us as we similarly desire to inspire others with this compilation. Gene Lorenz of St. Anthony's Publishing and his colleagues David Webster and Mike Grambo provided invaluable expert advice for which we are very grateful. We are also indebted to Andrea Heaton and Troy Brandt who contributed brilliantly and graciously on book design and layout, and Anne Kelley Conklin and Larry Harrison who provided expert copyediting and indexing skills respectively.

INDEX

Index

Barnes, Donald
    empathy, 10
    research animals, 75-76
Barron, R. A., 103
Barter, Gwendolen, 129-130
Basil, Saint, 49
Batt, Eva V., 49
battery hens. *See* chickens
Bayly, M. Beddow, 76
bears, 43-44, 136
beavers, 145-146
beef. *See* cows; meat consumption
Beeson, Paul B., 76
Bell, Ernest
    meat consumption, 50
    vegetarianism, 49-50
Bentham, Jeremy, 10
Berman, Phillip, 33
Bernard, Claude, 76-77
Berry, Father Thomas
    genetic engineering, 117
    nature, 117
    vegetarianism, 50
Besant, Annie, 23
Beston, Henry, 10-11
Bible, The
    divine compassion, 11
    and hunting, 130
    meat consumption, 50
    religious teachings, 33-34, 50
    respect for nature, 117
    souls of animals, 33-34
    treatment of animals, 11
Bigelow, Henry J., 77
Biggle, Lloyd, Jr., 11
Binkowski, Gloria J., 95
biology instruction. *See* dissection in education
Bird, Larry, 130
birds, 27, 31, 35, 42-44, 70, 121, 124, 136
Blake, Amanda, 144
Bloom, Joyce, 95-96
Bonaventure, Saint, 34

souls like ourselves

estrogen (Premarin) production, 69
ethics, 9-20
    and fur, 143-146
    Golden Rule, 42, 46-47, 58-59, 60
    indifference, 19
    and kinship, 13, 23, 25, 30
    and meat consumption, 50-62
    non-violence, 9, 12, 18, 19, 36
    obligation to protect the weak, 4, 9, 16, 23, 109, 112-113
    religious basis, 39, 43
    respect for life, 45
    and vivisection, 76-80, 76-91
evolution, theory of, 26, 46
exhibitions. *See* aquariums; bullfighting; circuses; greyhounds; movies; rodeos; zoos
experimentation on animals. *See* vivisection
exploitation of animals, 60
extrapolation, 81, 83-86, 88-92
Eysenck's Personality Questionnaire, 102

F
factory farms, 65-72
    dairy, 49, 65, 71-72
    ecological effects of, 55
    economics of, 66
    estrogen (Premarin) production, 69, 70-71
    and food safety, 49, 53
    Humane Farming Association, The, 72
    and Jewish tradition, 39
    pigs, 68, 70
    poultry, 65, 67-71
    veal production, 68, 69-70
Fano, Alix, 80
Farnum, George R., 12-13
fatherhood. *See* parenthood
fawns, 30, 43-44, 129
Fawver, A. L., 98
Felthous, Alan R., 110
feminism and animal activism, 166, 167
Ferrier, J. Todd, 53
Fiscella, Robert, 80
Fish and Wildlife Service, 149, 152-153

souls like ourselves

kosher slaughter, 39
Kowalski, Gary
      kinship, 27-28
      nature, 151
Krishnamurti, Jiddu
      changing society, 168
      nature, 121
Krutch, Joseph Wood
      hunting, 135
      nature, 121
      vivisection, 99
Kubacki, S. R., 81-82
Kundera, Milan, 15
Kunstler, William, 15
Kupfer, Edgar, 55-56

L
La Russa, Tony, 145
Laland, Stephanie
      furs and fur farming, 145-146
      parenthood, 151
Lambert, Florence L., 159
lambs, 51-52, 57
Landres, Lisa, 159
Langley, Gill, 28
Lantos, Tom, 83-84
Larson, Peggy, 159
law and legislation, 167-168, 169, 173
      animal cruelty laws, 15, 108, 149
      farm animal exclusion, 72
      toxicology standards, 84-85
LD50 values, 91-92
Leachman, Cloris, 56
Leadbeater, Charles W., 40
Leaning, Jennifer
      nature, 121-122
      vivisection, 91
      vivisection in education, 103
Lecky, W. E. H.
      ethics, 15
      meat consumption, 56-57
Lederberg, Joshua, 84

souls like ourselves

souls like ourselves

turtles, 96
Twain, Mark, 173

U

Ulrich, Roger, 89-90
unity of creation. *See* kinship; reverence for life
US Fish and Wildlife Service, 149, 152-153
Utopianism, 57

V

Van Buren, Abigail, 90
VanLooy, H. M., 90
veal production, 65, 68-71
vegetarianism, 49-62
        ecological benefits of, 55, 62, 122, 124
        health benefits of, 51, 52, 54, 55, 58, 59
video games, 115
violence. *See* aggression; domestic violence; non-violence
vivisection, 9, 75-92. *See also* dissection in education
        alternatives, 76, 80, 83, 86
        attitude of scientists, 81, 85-86, 88, 101
        ban in Argentina, 95
        vs. carcinogenic pollution, 79
        vs. chemical testing, 80
        comparative "value," 78, 82, 91
        compassion for animals, 84
        cosmetics testing, 79, 90
        as cowardice, 78
        economic motivation for, 79, 80
        in education, 96, 99-104
        effects on researchers, 81, 85-86, 89-90
        extrapolation to humans, 81, 83-86, 88-92
        vs. human studies, 80
        moral bankruptcy of, 84, 86-89
        need for restrictions, 88
        psychological experiments, 87
        and public disillusionment, 83-84
        quality of research, 81-82, 87
        and religion, 81
        suffering of animals, 82, 84, 86
        value of results, 83, 84, 85, 89, 90

souls like ourselves

souls like ourselves